GAME BOY ESSENTIALS VOLUME III

by Pierre-Luc Gagné

Game Boy Essentials Volume III

© 2019 - 2023 by Pierre-Luc Gagné

gameboyessentials.com

First Edition

This book is set in Adobe Caslon Pro, with Inconsolata for monospaced segments, and Avenir Next for headings. It also uses fonts from *Super Mario Land* and *Pokémon* for flourishes.

ISBN 978-0-9959015-8-2

To Annie, who I love as much as the Game Boy.
Almost.

Table of Contents

Introduction

It took way longer than expected, but I have completed another twelve articles, collected here for your enjoyment. I want to thank you; there aren't many of you reading me but I'm grateful to have found a small audience.

Volume 3 is the book with the most interesting collection of games yet. We have my favourite Game Boy title: *Dragon Warrior III*. There are two fascinating *kusoge* games: *The Simpsons: Itchy and Scratchy—Miniature Golf Madness* and *3D Pocket Pool*. We cap off the book with a long discussion of *Game Boy Camera*, the hottest digital camera of 1998. Oh, there's also this little game no one's heard of called *Pokémon*.

At this point, I feel like I'm hitting my stride and the limits of this project at the same time. This collection of articles is my best yet, while at the same time the format is showing its limits. There are sometimes many things outside the game I want to discuss, but I still have to maintain the premise that I'm talking about just one specific game. This forces me to get creative. I hope you'll appreciate my attempts to square the circle and provide you with an honest take on the game while at the same time talking about the larger history and context that surrounds the title being discussed. *Pokémon* was a particularly difficult game to wrap my head around. I hope you enjoy this book.

P.S: *Super Mario Land 2: Six Golden Coins* is included in this book while it was also in the first edition of Volume II. Due to an error on my part, the article on *Motocross Maniacs* was not included in Volume II and *Mario Land 2* was included instead. The second edition of Volume II solves this problem. Sorry!

Super Mario Land 2: 6 Golden Coins

- Japanese release in October 1992
- North American release in November 1992
- European release in 1993
- Published by Nintendo
- Developed by Nintendo R&D1

Isn't this cover awesome?

Weird

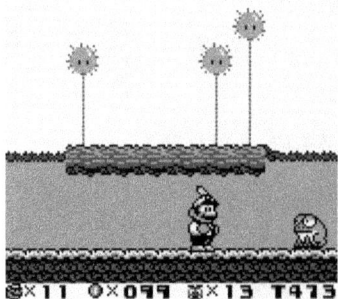

To me, nothing says summertime like *Super Mario Land 2: 6 Golden Coins*. I never had the game when I was a kid but my cousins did. Since I only saw them during the summer when our families would camp together on the family lot, I would borrow the game from them during the sunny summer months. Being a better player, I would get through the game unlocking for them the levels they couldn't reach. I was kind of the Game Boy idiot savant; all my cousins would dump their games on my lap to unlock stuff for them. In hindsight *Super Mario Land 2* is laughably easy. When you're a child though you have terrible hand-eye coordination. It makes everything more difficult but more interesting. Including this game.

And interesting it is! It's again, like the original *Super Mario Land*, made by Gunpei Yokoi's division in Nintendo. Let's get it out of the way: *Mario Land 2* is a great game. Lots of fun levels, plenty of interesting surprises, nothing is egregious with the game easy enough for everyone to enjoy. That being said, this game is weird on so many levels. It's essential to me for that: the many ways *Super Mario Land 2: 6 Golden Coins* is strange while staying a competent platformer worthy of the most recognizable video game character.

Weird Release

Super Mario Land 2: 6 Golden Coins is only the third game on Game Boy to have the name of Mario in the title: *Super Mario Land* and *Dr. Mario* are its two predecessors. So what was ultimately the most recognizable game character was seldom seen on Game Boy. He was featured as a guest character in many titles (he was the referee on the Game Boy version of *Tennis*, the paddle controller in *Alleyway*) but Nintendo really parcelled the release of Mario games. He was Miyamoto's character, and he oversaw all the major games featuring him. The team responsible for Mario clearly had no time to make Game Boy games (Miyamoto's EAD division was very busy making Super Nintendo titles) so it fell to R&D1 to use him on Game Boy.

Looking at *Super Mario Land 2*, I can't shake the idea that someone at Nintendo (most probably our favourite bespectacled supervilain Nintendo president, Hiroshi Yamauchi) told Gunpei Yokoi's team to put something like the brand new *Super Mario World* on Game Boy. The only Mario platformer on Game Boy was getting very long in the tooth by 1992: *Super Mario Land* was an analogue of *Super Mario Bros.* that used very small sprites. Read my article on *Super Mario Land* to read about its design. Suffice it to say, those smaller sprites were never impressive and platformers on Game Boy were now very successful at using console-sized sprites. Mario's time to grow up on Game Boy had clearly arrived.

A comparison between the *Land* sprites and the *Land 2* sprites.

The game is a sibling to *Super Mario World*, sure, but the fine people at Yokoi's R&D1 did not strictly ape the Super Nintendo title; they made a game all their own.

Weird Design

Each early Mario game has a very specific idea about its design. Since *Super Mario Land 2* is clearly meant to emulate *Super Mario World* on Super Nintendo, we have to look at its overarching idea about level design to understand what's happening. *Super Mario World* was built on the idea that you are exploring a strange new land, Dinosaur Land, taking the time to discover new challenges and enemy types. It might sound weird to think the game best remembered for its speedy cape acrobatics and running with Yoshi is ultimately about a leisurely stroll but that's really what the game is about. Compare the game with its predecessor: in *Super Mario Bros. 3* you have eight worlds and the levels within those eight worlds are all of a similar type. Each world is thus a theme. But there are weird outliers, levels which seem disconnected from the overarching theme of the world. And the levels are very short. You don't really feel like you're exploring, discovering. You're going through a gauntlet of short, themed challenges. And this fits within the conceit of *Super Mario Bros. 3* that Mario and Co. are acting out a play. That the platforms are stage-play elements bolted on to the background. That you're fighting against a bolted-on level, not a functioning cartoon environment. *Super Mario World* has a more deliberate pace, putting you in gameplay situations that last for a longer period of time. They obviously decided to implement fewer ideas, but explore those ideas more. The levels are long, usually have one single gameplay idea and explore that idea to a natural conclusion. *Super Mario Land 2* is trying to do a very similar thing. This more deliberate pace, slower exploration of a gameplay idea lent itself very well to the Game Boy. R&D1 could use this idea, make Mario and his enemies' sprites bigger and build a world that felt fun to traverse with such big sprites compared to the previous *Mario Land* game.

Weird Camera

I've been fascinated since the beginning of this project by the choices developers made to address the Game Boy's limited resolution. What did R&D1 do to deal with a bigger

Mario sprite? They basically did what every other developer had done and made the camera move during jumps while adapting the world around your character to better fit this bigger character.

Since the camera moves with every jump, it produces ghosting with everything on the screen. There's no escaping it, but since you already get ghosting from horizontal movement, we all lived with it. To alleviate the ghosting the backgrounds are kept simple. There's no big secret to it; you'll get ghosting on every pixel from any scrolling so you have to keep a healthy dose of whitespace. The other, less obvious thing they did to reduce the impact of ghosting is keeping hazards far apart from one another. Enemies don't gather, they don't hang around together in groups, they're each and every one of them pretty much alone. So much so that you tend to have only one enemy on the screen at a time. Console Mario games oftentimes have situations where you'll jump from enemy to enemy to clear a hole or a hazard. It does not happen in *Super Mario Land 2*.

Gauntlets of multiple varied enemies simply do not exist in this game.

It's not a strict rule, but it's clearly intentional; hazards tend to be far from one another to give you ample time to decipher and react to them. You don't want to have to try and make sense of a giant glob of ghosting, you want to have to figure out a **small** glob of ghosting. It definitely helps with the smaller resolution of the screen but it's not perfect; I distinctly remember having a hard time *reading* enemies in *Mario Land 2* when I was a kid who had only seen the game through a DMG's screen. But it made sense, Mario on Game Boy finally looked like every other platformer on Game Boy instead of being a weird outlier. I mean, Mario went from using four pixels for his nose to an impressive twelve whole pixels. Twelve!

Weird Style

The jump from four pixels to twelve for Mario's nose (twelve!) is emblematic of what they did to our beloved plumber's world. The small team of developers at R&D1 were no longer stuck trying to make iconic Mario enemies and locales work in such a small size. They could artistically interpret the characters and environments that made Mario famous. In *Super Mario Land*, Goombas looked like the shadow of a Goomba. In this game they have a sprite big enough to convey a specific style. They have big eyes and eyebrows; they're really expressive.

The enemies they created are weird. It's a cavalcade of enemies that don't fit. Vampires, sharks, the three little pigs, chibi Jason, the torture ball Vader uses on Leia in *Star Wars*, everything that doesn't make sense in a Mario game is there, mixed in with the classic enemies. Miyamoto's Mario lives in a cohesive Disney cartoon; R&D1 put him in a Don Bluth production! Ultimately, it's not a major issue. You just accept the weirdness, and you roll with it. But upon closer inspection it does feel out of place. Hindsight is twenty-twenty but it feels to me like they were hitching for the satirical approach to character design that permeates *Wario Land*. The bug-eyed bird you fight on top of Tree Zone looks like the son of the vulture from *Wario Land*.

Mario Land 2 feels looser, less laser-focused than the other Mario games. The controls are floaty and extremely forgiving. It clearly was not made by Miyamoto, the master of laser focus.

Weird World-Building

By 1992, Mario was finally a properly managed brand. Gone were the heady days of Captain Lou Albano or the crappy Donkey Kong cartoons of the '80s. Mario was still reeling from those strange decisions for sure. Reruns of those shows ran everywhere and pallets of the disgusting (from what I've heard) cereal were still hanging about. The imbecilic *Super Mario Bros.* movie starring Bob Hoskins would not come out until 1993. But the worse was over: the brand managers at Nintendo were reeling from all the misplaced trust they put into other creators and would not make the same mistake again. And again. And again. I mean, let me stop my train of thought for a second to highlight how many **terrible** people were entrusted with the golden goose. The aforementioned cereal made by Ralston Purina (the same company as the animal food). The terrible toys made by Nasta, a toy maker so forgotten it doesn't have a Wikipedia article or a mention on websites dedicated to 80s toys. DiC's cavalcade of cheaply made cartoons, written by old men who couldn't care less about Mario.

The point I was making was that all the people at Nintendo had finally seen Mario for what he really was: a global icon who needs to be managed like the biggest star in the world. Whitney Houston doesn't participate in shitty low-budget kid shows with washed-out wrestlers. Why should Mario? They finally realized he's above that (or the Nintendo headquarters in Japan forced the people at Nintendo of America to come to grips with that fact) so it gradually stopped. But what about the people making the games?

There is obviously now a coordinated effort to get Mario in high-quality productions. Mario is not above being in other companies' games. Think of the Olympic-branded games from Sega and *Mario + Rabbids Kingdom Battle*. They clearly have to be of a certain type: they're either the franchises that have existed for a long time (the sports games, *Itadaki Street*, *Mario Party*) or very high quality. But what about the internal Nintendo teams?

Daddy gets a pass. The people reporting to Miyamoto at EAD can do whatever they want with the little dude. They put Mario in a go-kart, they started him golfing. But what about the other teams? That's where we land at *Super Mario Land 2*. It was made by people at R&D1, who never reported to Miyamoto. It features weird out-of-place elements, just like the first *Super Mario Land*. Cheeky sharks. Bug-eyed birds. A level featuring the Lego ripoff R&D1 made in the '60s, the N&B blocks. A whole zone that's a giant statue of Mario himself (with a level filled with balls right in the crotch of Mario's statue). Nothing fits with the modern look of the Mushroom Kingdom because the game did not have Shigeru Miyamoto's point of view of what fits in a Mario game.

The closest feeling is New Donk City in *Super Mario Odyssey*. Even though Odyssey was made with Miyamoto, I'd argue they did something that did not obey their own internal logic when Mario exists next to correctly proportioned humans who tower above him. Just like it makes no internal sense that there are cowfish swimming in sap inside a giant tree on Mario's private island.

There is, however, one thing that *Super Mario Land 2* did that is absolutely pinpoint on brand for Mario.

Weird Mario

Oh boy. Here comes the *Scoundrel with a Fart of Gold*, the garlic plumber himself: **WA-RI-O**! The despised mirror version of Mario is so fun to talk about. He's just so dumb as a character, but so profound as a concept. Wario is a postmodern critique on video games, an intra-office shitpost, an ambassador to the '90s gross-out movement, a vitriolic response to the success of Sonic the Hedgehog, a necessary reinvention of platforming concepts for the Game Boy, he is all of that and more.

Wario was created by Hiroji Kiyotake, who worked for R&D1, **not** EAD, and everything about him is a twisted reflexion on Mario. But we can't read too much into him from this game; he is seldom seen and simply amounts to evil Mario. He's mostly a copy of Bluto, Popeye's foil. Future games will embrace and expand his wonderfully terrible personality with wonderful results. Here, it's actually Mario's role who's subversive. It's the first time since *Donkey Kong Jr.* that Mario is not doing something altruistic. He's rescuing his own private island, complete with a gigantic statue of himself. To the people at R&D1, Mario's an entitled asshole, with his own private fiefdom devoted to his own inflated ego. Who the hell could *cough* Miyamoto *cough* that represent?

Wario, the R&D1 creation, is a greedy goof who played with Mario's stuff until the ultimate sourdough comes to put an end to his fun.

Conclusion

There clearly were good ideas among the fine people who made this game, but using Mario was holding them back. Next time they made a platformer, they changed their protagonist. They instead made a game starring the brand new villain of *Mario Land 2*, a character the marketing department and R&D1 both fell in love with: Wa-ri-o! We all would fall in love with Wario in due time.

Game & Watch Gallery

- Japanese release in February 1997
- North American release in May 1997
- European release in August 1997
- Published by Nintendo
- Developed by Nintendo R&D1

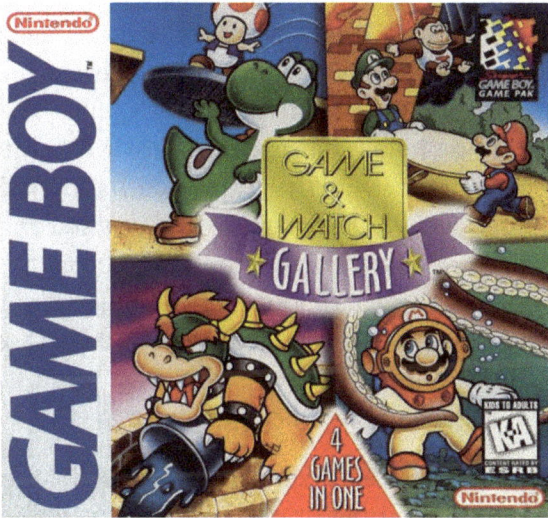

Welcome once again to the world of Game & Watch!

Re-Revisited

For years, my local game store had, behind its glass case, a *Donkey Kong* Game & Watch unit for sale for around forty-five dollars. Compared to prices you find online, this felt reasonable. I would look at it every time from behind the glass case, just admiring it. One day, I got bold and asked the employee if I could hold it. That was a mistake; once I had held the Game & Watch in my hands, I was hooked. Even though it had no batteries so I could not play it, just holding it in my hands really shook me; this was not what I was envisioning. I expected a device completely divorced from other Nintendo portables. Quite the contrary. It felt like I was holding a smaller, flimsier DS Lite. Peering over it, I saw defects that explained its low price. The metal top had lots of scratch marks and was starting to peel off. When open, it was missing both its decorated bottom panels. One of the metal inserts for the hinge was missing. The plastic clip to keep it closed was broken. All of those problems were minor. The store employee promised me it worked, and they've always been trustworthy.

I discovered many surprising things while holding it. The console is very small but sturdy. It does not feel cheap in your hands. Like I said, it even has a metal sheet on the top cover with the logos. The Game Boy never used metal for the exterior casing! It does not feel cheap, but instead feels made using economical engineering. The best example is the hinge of the device. You have the bottom and top kept together by a round metal piece inside two simple plastic hinges. But that simple hinge does not allow an electric connection between the top and bottom parts, which is needed for the second display on the top. So how did they get the signal through? They simply passed the display's flex cable through thin slits, exposing it to the elements. The cable is somewhat protected between the two bulkier hinges, and unless you jab at the flex cable you're not going to break it. This is incredible due to its simplicity. Another cost-saving measure is the battery housing. It's very simple, with no spring to hold the batteries in place, or a screw to keep it closed. If you slide the plastic cover, the batteries come flying out, and you lose your set alarm and top score. Nintendo included small stickers in the boxes to put on the cover and prevent a curious kid from opening it. It's not strong childproofing, but it has the benefit of being cheaper than a screw.

I could not put the little machine back in the display case after holding it; the Game & Watch had seduced me. I happily paid for it and put it where it felt the most appropriate; in my coat's breast pocket. I then stopped at a big chain store to buy its frankly esoteric button cells (two LR44 batteries, if you must know) and went home.

My *Donkey Kong* Game & Watch.

I put the tiniest tie wrap I could find to hold the two pieces of the plastic hinge. The front panels, which looked like they were initially glued on the front plastic, don't affect the experience. I know what they looked like, and the unit is fully functional without them.

I have to say, I initially thought the electronics were broken. The batteries were so foreign to me that I put them in backwards. By the way, those small watch batteries **can kill you** if you swallow them. They leak their acid in your stomach and intestine. Keep them out of reach of children! I finally figured out the batteries, and the system came to life.

The initial box for the American release.

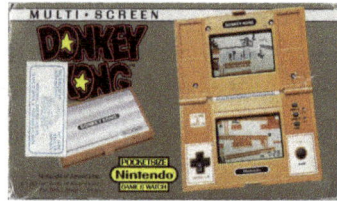

The back of the box, with the label of a Montréal toy store!

Nintendo later sold Game & Watch devices through third parties. Nintendo would never design such a terrible blister pack.

Or that one.

At last. A watch that's fun.

In the UK, Nintendo even sold their Game & Watch games through CGL, which rebadged LCD games from multiple companies.

To get some context, start by watching the Japanese TV ad for Oil Panic and Donkey Kong. It's interesting to see how they were marketed, and that they each cost the equivalent of 25 US dollars in 1982, around 50 USD today. The first thing that captures my attention is Nintendo's steadfast commitment to making all Game & Watch systems a functioning clock. Turning it on for the first time presents you with a blinking 12:00, imploring you to set its time. It is literally in the name (Game & *Watch*), and I guess you can use the system as an alarm clock on your bedside, but it is somewhat surprising. Equally surprising is the lack of any volume control. No mute, no nothing. Considering this device was meant to be played during a busy commute, I'm puzzled as to the absence of those controls. I'm sure many Game & Watch devices had their speaker wires cut by savvy parents wanting a moment of silence.

The gameplay is sublime because it's designed in lockstep with the limited display. That is the strongest point of praise you can give a Game & Watch. I have talked at length in previous articles about the limited nature of the Game Boy's screen. The Game & Watch's liquid crystal display is even more primitive. It is the same limited technology that you will find in a pocket calculator.

Since a calculator display has no discrete pixels, only segmented elements to turn on or off, you need to design your game around the constraint that no two elements can ever overlap. Imagine it in the context of the Game & Watch I own, *Donkey Kong*. In the arcade, Donkey Kong throws barrels that roll down the girders; the very same girders that Mario walks on. When you get hit by a barrel, it's because Mario physically touched a barrel. No such thing can happen on the Game & Watch version. Your character stands on the girders in fifteen discrete positions, but you can't have the barrels intersect your character. The decision made here was to put them very close to the side of the player character. And here comes the Nintendo R&D1 touch: there is a delay between the barrel appearing right next to your character and the barrel hitting you in that position. They implemented a slight delay before you get hit to account for the barrel's rolling! They are working with your imagination of the barrel's movement, which gives you the ability to jump above the barrel just like the arcade game.

On the bottom screen, you are dealing with barrels, but since the technology cannot properly render the frenetic barrel action of the arcade *Donkey Kong*, the developers added one more challenge than just the barrels. You also have girders on cranes above your head that can kill you if you jump. Once you clear those challenges, you have a ladder to ascend to reach the top screen. Girders can hit you on the way up, and barrels can hit you at the top of the ladder. Once you reach the very top, you are right underneath Donkey Kong, who has been throwing all the barrels you have been encountering. He moves from left to right, and throws barrels straight down. His arms are different segments from the rest of his body so he moves, picks up a barrel, and then throws it, and all those actions are separate and clearly telegraphed. On the top screen, you have to push a switch, and then jump right to reach a crane, while dodging Donkey's barrels. You have to jump to hit the crane, which swings left and right. This means you can miss it and lose a life. Each time you reach the crane, you get to remove a bolt from Donkey's platform. Remove all four bolts and Donkey falls headfirst on the ground. You then repeat from the start.

The controls to achieve all these actions are wonderful. Other dedicated consoles of the time were not known for their great controls, but Nintendo always stood above the rest. There are some issues; the Jump button is made of soft rubber instead of the expected plastic, and the reset buttons are very small and recessed inside the case. They're meant more for your nail than your finger. However, the star of the show is the directional controller, the Plus Button.

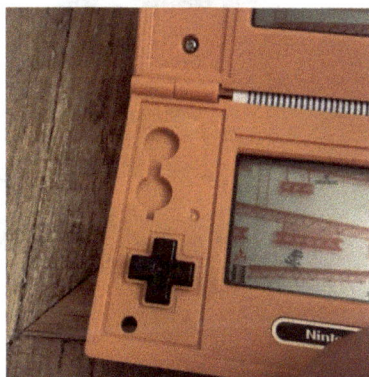

Now known as the D-Pad, the *Donkey Kong* Game & Watch is literally what it was invented for. The people at R&D1 needed a way to bring the joystick of the arcade to a portable machine; their solution was so natural we could not imagine video games without it anymore. All previous Game & Watch games required at most four buttons to play, which back then they simply made into separate buttons on both sides of the display. You then covered all the buttons with your thumbs and pressed with your fingertip for the top button and your joint for the bottom one. But to adequately convey the action of the arcade *Donkey Kong*, you need the four cardinal directions *and* jump. Since no one has three thumbs, they needed a new control system for the game. Could they have simply put a small arcade stick on the system? That's what Coleco did.

A Coleco tabletop game.

But Coleco's licensed game was a tabletop; you did not fold it nor hold it while playing, you merely set it down on a table. This meant it was possible to grasp the stick with the two required fingers with the system safely stable on a table. Nintendo could not do the same as Coleco. It was not reasonable to have you hold a Game & Watch while you manipulate a mini arcade stick. It's far from ideal. So only something flat for your thumb would do, since the rest of your palm is used to hold the Game & Watch. Their solution was to flatten the arcade stick. They put a plus sign on a small ball above the four buttons. Press on the pad in one direction, and the D-Pad will push the button you want with the contact pad underneath the button creating the contact. What this means in practice is that your thumb is not managing four separate buttons but just one. Your thumb rests in the middle of the pad and moves in the direction you want to press. The Plus button is, to put it simply, genius. Nintendo patented the shit out of it, which meant everybody had to invent an inferior method to implement their own D-Pads.

I do ultimately feel a bit stupid explaining a D-Pad, since it's so ubiquitous but sometimes we need to explain easy stuff because we take it for granted. I ultimately feel privileged to own a *Donkey Kong* Game & Watch, since I own the first D-Pad ever made. It's smaller than an NES D-Pad, but unless you know it's the first one ever made, you would never suspect it. The wizards at R&D1 got it right the first time.

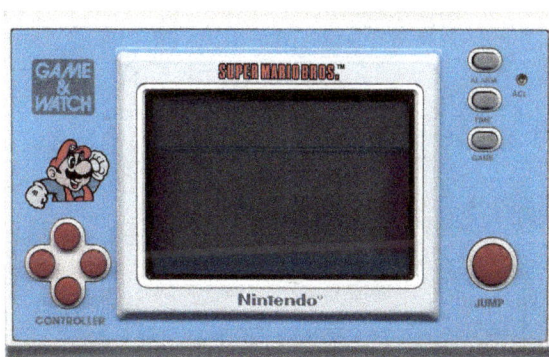

Strangely, they would not use a D-Pad for every future Game & Watch units. Only lids that closed and could protect it got one. This later *Super Mario Bros.* game got a terrible controller that looks like a Switch's dreaded D-Pad.

A Slow Start

Moving on to recreations of Game & Watch portables, right when you first start *Game & Watch Gallery*, you can feel the energy that went into making this game. A big Mario sprite comes in to chill out on the front screen. An animated sprite this big means real efforts were spent on this game. They broke from the staid look of *Game Boy Gallery*. When Nintendo puts Mario in a game, it's meant as a mark of quality.

And some of Nintendo's best talent were working on this game. Two managers at Nintendo, Yamagami Hitoshi and Izushi Takehiro worked as director and producer respectively. You even have Tezuka Takashi, the genius designer behind Miyamoto's greatest games, helping out as an advisor. It seems most of the lower level staff were TOSE employees. Direct oversight of those contractors by three Nintendo employees meant that their collective efforts would be spent making the game good; they succeeded at making the general concept of the game much better than Nintendo's last Game & Watch collection, *Game Boy Gallery*.

Classic and Modern

The secret to Nintendo's improvement: the Modern and Classic dichotomy. *Game Boy Gallery* offered new graphics but the same gameplay as the original game. Here, we instead have two distinct modes. First, a faithful recreation of the original game called the Classic Mode. Second, a reinvention of the game with new sound, gameplay, and graphics using characters related to the Mario franchise called the Modern Mode.

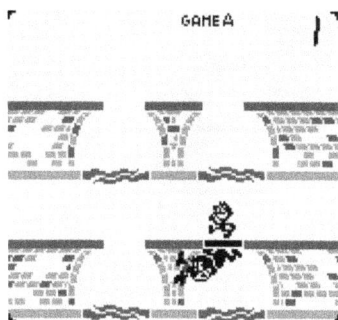
Classic *Manhole*

Modern *Manhole*

Classic *Fire*

Modern *Fire*

Classic *Octopus*

Modern *Octopus*

Game & Watch Gallery

Classic *Oil Panic*   Modern *Oil Panic*

The modern versions all have new bells and whistles. For example, the modern version of *Octopus* slows downs Mario if he has collected more treasure. This introduces an element of gambling; should I keep plundering, knowing that I will be slowed down significantly when going back to the surface? This variable walking speed is possible because Mario visibly walks between the discrete points of the ocean floor. He simply walks slower between them when carrying a heavier load. This detailed mechanic was impossible with the LCD screen of a Game & Watch.

Stars and Unlocking

Another improvement that the game has over *Game Boy Gallery* are unlockable rewards. You receive a star every 200 points you accumulate in all the game modes, for a maximum of five stars per mode. With each game having four modes (Classic A and B, Modern Easy and Hard), you have a ton of star gathering to get through.

As a reward for accruing stars, you can unlock viewable versions of Game & Watch games with a short paragraph about the game. Emphasis on *viewable*. The games are not playable, contrary to what you will read online. This confusion is widespread, and baffling.

How You'll Play

The game flow for me is somewhat frustrating. Since you want to get stars, you need to play all the easy modes, but they are so easy they're boring. I end up not paying enough attention because I'm bored, and I start making mistakes. Since the games reset their speed when you lose one of your three lives, I get even more bored after a mistake because it becomes even easier. The harder modes are a bit better but they're still repetitive games. You still risk losing your focus and making mistakes. To alleviate that, I tend to play in shorter sessions. It's what I recommend; *Game & Watch Gallery* is better played in fifteen to twenty-minute increments.

Interrupt Save

You'll want to play in such short bursts, and the developers have thought about it too. They designed a wonderful feature to save your progress; the game offers what it calls interrupt saves. If you pause a game, turn off your Game Boy, and turn it back on again, the game will allow you to continue where you left off. It achieves this magic trick by saving your game every time you press Start. To the modern player, this might feel like save states. However these cannot be used for save scumming since the save disappears the moment you resume your game. You have no ability to preserve a previous save. I had no idea that this functionality existed when I was a kid, since I could not read the English explanation. It took me a long time to figure out how sometimes when I turned on the console it allowed me to start a game in progress.

Had I been able to read English, I would have gotten an explanation through the game's hint system. Periodically, the game will give you hints about different aspects of the game.

Quality

I have to admit, as I wrap up, that I am a bit underwhelmed by the games on display here. I have played *Game & Watch Gallery 2* a lot when I was a kid, and my experience of this first title is inevitably tainted by the sequel. The four games on offer here are fine, but their modern versions are all too close to the classic versions. They are all additive versions and not reinventions. *Game & Watch Gallery 2* offers a more eclectic selection. Games like *Vermin* will change the perspective and the fail state of the classic version; only the player action will remain the same. This variety will make the sequel a much better game.

Conclusion

Playing a Game & Watch explains so clearly how Nintendo approached the Game Boy. Their main competitor, Sega, produced a portable version of their somewhat successful 8-bit Master System console. NEC did the same thing by making a portable PC Engine. R.J. Mical and Dave Needle designed what would become the Atari Lynx based on their experience designing the powerful Amiga computers. All those portable consoles featured colour screens, large plastic housings, high prices and abysmal battery life. Nintendo, ever the outlier, instead looked to expand from its diminutive Game & Watch line. It chose to use a shockingly limited screen, coupled with a CPU architecture known for its low-power qualities, to achieve an impressive fifteen to twenty hours of battery life with a competitive price. Where the competition tried to cram TV experiences into your palm with battery-guzzling failures, Nintendo R&D1 simply evolved their best-in-class Game & Watch experiences for battery-sipping success.

No wonder they were so reverential to their Game & Watch games, trying twice to update them for the Game Boy. Those games were the true ancestors of Nintendo's Game Boy. Their second attempt at redefining those games was clearly a success and with their next collection they would reach surprising heights.

The Australian cover. If you remember my article about *Game Boy Gallery*, you'll remember why this game is a sequel in Australia.

The Simpsons: Itchy and Scratchy – Miniature Golf Madness

- North American release in November 1994
- European release in 1994
- Never Released in Japan
- Published by Acclaim
- Developed by Beam Software

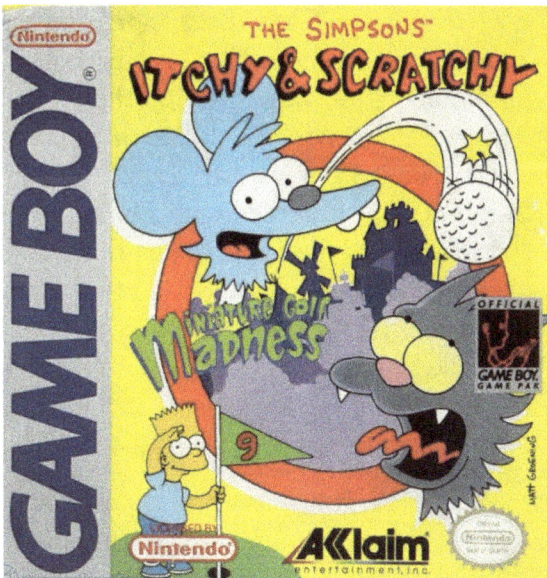

Wow! Free balloons for everyone who enters.

They Drove a Dump Truck Full of Money Up to My House!

The year 1994 is the sad middle age of Game Boy. It seemed the console was dying of neglect back then. Few games were released, and they're mostly forgettable, since most releases were tie-in games for projects and franchises who bothered to release on Game Boy because if you wanted to be on every popular console you had to be on Game Boy. Nobody could fathom that the console was due for an enormous comeback, so it looked like all the must-play games had already been released. I would say no more than five great games were released in 1994 on Game Boy. Of course the Super Game Boy was released that year, but it did nothing to help the Game Boy's moribund years since it wasn't a game, and its marketing heavily focused on the ability to play **older** titles. Case in point, the cover of Super Game Boy's box featured *Metroid II: Return of Samus*, a game from 1991. Of course, 1994 was the year of the masterpiece *Donkey Kong* (not to be confused with *Donkey Kong Land*), released to coincide with the Super Game Boy, but one masterpiece amongst a sea of deplorable games was not enough. The perception that the Game Boy was in its twilight, that Nintendo was likely working on a successor to their portable console, was everywhere.

The Simpsons: Itchy and Scratchy — Miniature Golf Madness is born of this era. It is a forgettable tie-in title focused on the cartoon-within-a-cartoon ultraviolent parody of *Tom & Jerry* that Bart loves on *The Simpsons*. Acclaim held the licence for *The Simpsons* video games and the company published underwhelming titles from multiple developers. All their Simpsons games were terrible, no matter who developed them. The exception that confirms the rule is Konami's arcade game, but I don't think that Acclaim ever had anything to do with Konami's arcade licence.

It was a well-known quantity that Simpsons games were trash amongst my friends; one should never rent or buy a Simpsons game, they're awful. The interesting part is that I had never rented any NES Simpsons game myself. It was schoolyard knowledge that was imparted on me. Once, however, I remember a friends' older brother had rented *The Simpsons: Bart vs. the World* on NES. I was at his house and he was playing the first level, which had Bart on a Chinese boat.

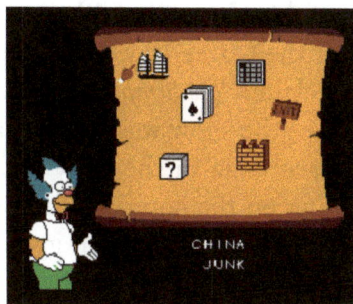

The first level is called junk. It's like they knew.

The level was backward from the usual NES fare: you had to go left instead of right. I still vividly remember the older brother going right and falling straight into the water and dying. He then went left with his next life and got immediately killed by a dynamite stick. Then something broke inside of him. I think he knew then and there that *Bart vs. the World* was a shitty game, and he was having none of it. He spent his remaining lives jumping in the water as fast as he could to get to a Game Over screen. I asked him what was wrong. He simply replied that the game was broken, got up, and brought the game back to the convenience store where he had rented it. He managed to convince the store to change his rental for another game.

Remembering that story got me thinking about video game rental stores of yesteryear. Did clerks know which games were terrible based on the amount of time it took to bring them back, thoroughly pissed off?

> No, don't rent the new *Bartman Meets Radioactive Man*. We've just received it yesterday, but any Simpsons game is always a guaranteed forty-five minute return.

With all this emotional baggage towards games based on *The Simpsons*, I can't say I expect much out of *Itchy and Scratchy—Miniature Golf Madness*. Especially considering the double whammy of this Game Boy title game being released in the doldrums of the Game Boy, and it being itself a doldrum release of Acclaim's *The Simpsons* licence deal. Acclaim held the licence since the show was popular, and they clearly benefitted from Bartmania in the early '90s. They did the clever thing of riding on the popularity of Bart. He was the hot new thing, and they marketed their games as Bart games more than anything else. Bart fight aliens, Bart somehow fights the world. The other Simpsons characters were irrelevant. They stooped so low as to eventually make a game about Bartman, a five-second gag whose only benefit was that it sounded cool in concept. By 1994, when they released this game, Bartmania was over and the show was still relevant, but was far from the most talked about show on TV. The people at Acclaim were willing to try weirder things with their licence. They did *Virtual Bart* on SNES and Genesis. They somehow published *The Simpsons: Bart and the Beanstalk* on Game Boy a couple of months earlier. Why not try a mini-putt game featuring the cartoon characters that Bart loves?

I Sure Hope Someone Got Fired for That Blunder

Let's start the game. You get through the menus and start playing the game. You are playing as Scratchy, in what looks like a side-scrolling platformer. In front of you is a ball, which makes the game somewhat unique: a side-scrolling golf game is not a regular occurrence. So you try to hit that ball, and oh boy! When you press the B button Scratchy swings a club **and the ball jumps up a bit without moving forward.**

I finally managed to figure out what is wrong, but it took forever! The game uses the B button as an attack. You're supposed to use your attack against Itchy. Since you haven't even seen Itchy yet, you don't know that. If you hit the ball with that attack it will react by jumping straight up. To get into your golfing stance, you need to press Up right next to the ball. So the game is about hitting a golf ball through a hole while dodging Itchy sprites. You pick up weapons to hit Itchy, but the dastardly mouse constantly reappears. There is therefore no point in attacking it since it is infinitely reappearing. You're better simply jumping over Itchy and letting it go across the screen. You can then safely get back to the crappy mini-putt the game offers. You hit the ball a couple of times, try to clear a hill or a hole, jump over Itchy. Get a small chuckle out of the gigantic Krusty head.

As a gameplay loop, it sucks. I've had enough playing one level. I do not need to play more of this useless game.

I feel like Game Boy players back then came to the same conclusion as me. Even with such anemic new releases, players had better options on Game Boy than what was newly released in 1994. Older classics could still be found, and if you move forward in time to 1996 after the failure of the Virtual Boy, Nintendo used the Player's Choice rereleases as a way to put good titles back on store shelves. Even during the doldrums years before the one-two punch of *Pokémon* and the Game Boy Color revitalized the Game Boy in 1998, you could still find excitement. You just had to skew towards older titles.

Conclusion

I do not believe that this terrible Itchy and Scratchy game needs to be tried at Nuremberg, but there must be a smaller venue for German war criminals where we could prosecute the game. All joking aside, there is no value whatsoever to be gained from *playing* the game. It simply exists as a marketing vehicle, released near the end of Acclaim's licence, meant to find a new vein of interest with *The Simpsons* in the sleepy doldrums of Game Boy's history. Its historical value lies in its marketing during a tough year for both the Game Boy and games based on *The Simpsons*. For that, however, it is interesting. Those tough years existed for multiple reasons, and gave us a couple of years where it was hard to look at a rack of new releases and feel excited. The developers who made this game were simply asked to provide something cheap that featured *Itchy & Scratchy*. That was enough to merit the release it got.

I'D NEVER LEND MY NAME TO AN INFERIOR PRODUCT.

The Simpsons writers knew all the way back during Bartmania that the brand was being used for terrible products; they knew so they made fun of it.

Donkey Kong Land 2

- North American release in September 1996
- Japanese release in November 1996
- European release in November 1996
- Published by Nintendo
- Developed by Rare

An exciting cover for an unfortunate sequel.

Ape Escape

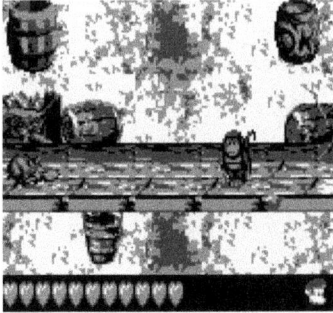

My article on *Donkey Kong Land* is by far my most popular. It's the one that has received the most feedback; from book reviews on Amazon, from Reddit's /r/gameboy, from talking to my friends. With that in mind, I should feel a certain responsibility discussing *Donkey Kong Land 2*. Since they barely changed anything, I don't. it's just talking about the same core mistakes all over again.

With the first game, I had decades of experience to share; I owned the game has a kid. This time, I bought the game as an adult, specifically for this project. Since I have never played the game before, it means my opinions are fresh. The game features only minuscule improvements on the issues I had with the first game, so I am disappointed to say I do not like this sequel. It stings particularly because this game tries to reproduce *Donkey Kong Country 2: Diddy's Kong Quest* for the Game Boy, and I simply adore *Donkey Kong Country 2*. I have fond memories of playing the game with my best friend from primary school, slowly inching our way, level by level, through this difficult Super Nintendo classic. *Donkey Kong Land 2* attempts to ape this seminal game and fails miserably. At least the first *Land* game had original levels. Essentially, we're faced here with the harsh fact that a bad adaptation of a great game is worse than a bad but original work.

Slightly Better on the eyes

The biggest issue with the first *Donkey Kong Land* is its inscrutable backgrounds that make everything blurry. The developers of *Donkey Kong Land 2* thought so too; the second game has somewhat cleaner backgrounds.

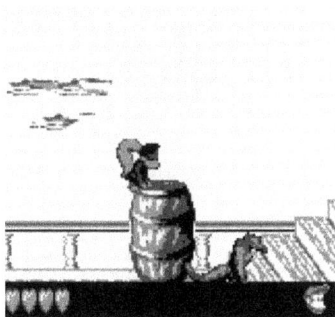

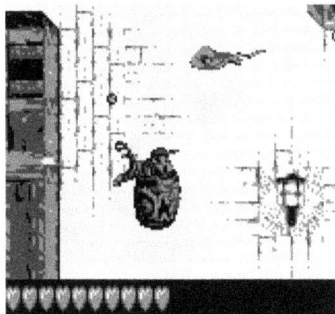

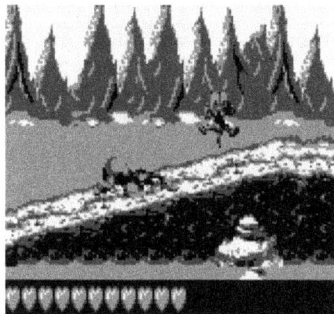

They evidently tried to alleviate the problem by using more whitespace but I think they were trying to improve a fundamentally flawed concept. There is no way to make 3D designs work flawlessly on the original Game Boy screen, no matter how much whitespace you're leaving in the background. They did not fully commit to the improvements; you still have many decorative elements that crush visibility throughout the game. You can better discern the position of the dark blobs that populate the screen, but you'll have a hard time figuring out what those blobs are supposed to be.

> Is this a background element or an enemy? It threw what looks like a barrel, so I guess it's an enemy? Oh, it wasn't a barrel, it was a cannonball so now I'm dead. Why don't I play some *Kirby's Dream Land 2* instead of this crap?

You need the clean lines of hand-drawn pixel art to give you a game you'll be able to see without issues. Since the whole marketing angle of the *Donkey Kong Country* series was its use of 3D graphics, they chose to use the same underlying technique on Game Boy. To hell with the game's quality.

Pocket Reinvention

Just like *Donkey Kong Land* was released to coincide with the arrival of the Super Game Boy on store shelves, *Donkey Kong Land 2* was released on the same day as the Game Boy Pocket. If we are supposed to understand that this game was made with the Game Boy Pocket in mind, I guess it solves its more egregious graphical issues, but we still must acknowledge all the poor players who did not own a Game Boy Pocket to play this bad game. I had to contend with my trusty grey brick until I bought a Game Boy Color in 2000, and I was not alone. For seven years the Game Boy had been sold to most everyone who wanted a Game Boy when the Game Boy Pocket was introduced in 1996. The Pocket did not sell particularly well nor change the Game Boy market significantly. It also raised the sale price of the Game Boy by $10 USD upon release. How come Nintendo improved their initial design only by 1996? Because during four of those seven years, Yokoi Gunpei and R&D1 were busy working on the Virtual Boy. Once they finally abandoned it on the market in 1995, Yokoi finally tasked his team with building a better Game Boy.

That the Game Boy Pocket came as the amends for the sins of Virtual Boy makes sense. Since their previous creation was too much of an overreach, they went in the opposite direction and the Game Boy Pocket is the safest redesign possible. Its marquee feature is the improved display, finally

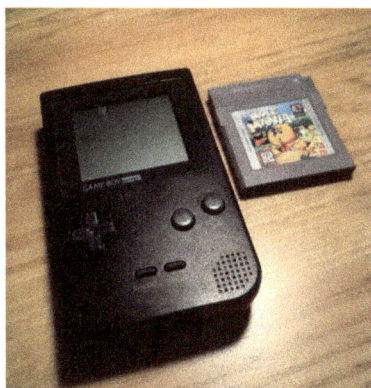

breaking from the shackles of the iconic green screen. The Game Boy Pocket still uses a super-twisted nematic LCD with all its faults, but it is much improved, with far less ghosting and true shades of grey. They also made the screen slightly bigger in physical size while keeping the same resolution. The screen has no light source, but that was still par for the course for a device sold for $70 USD in 1996. The overall device size is smaller, with a fresh, timeless design.

They were also able to only require two batteries, since between the release of the DMG in 1989 and the Pocket in 1996, a small revolution happened in the world of consumer electronics: the move from 5 V to 3 V. The crew at Nintendo R&D1 were able to make the Pocket work with 3 V, meaning that instead of the four batteries needed to reach 5 V (a single AA battery provides a nominal 1.5 V), you only needed two batteries to reach 3 V. On the negative side, they chose to use AAA batteries, which dropped the battery life of the Pocket to the 10-hour mark, while the original DMG usually gave

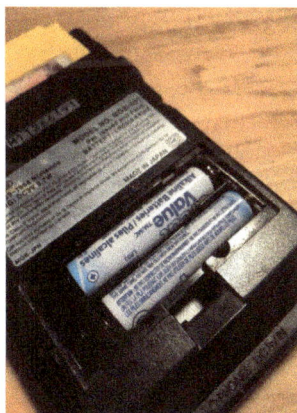

you 20 hours of gameplay with its AAs. No other Game Boy would ever use the diminutive AAA batteries again, and they would all offer more than 10 hours of battery life. All that to say that *Donkey Kong Land 2* had at its disposal a device better suited for its visuals, but it still doesn't make the game good.

Bad as a Portable Donkey Kong Country 2

You might be tempted to say: "Pierre-Luc, the first game was just a bizarre adaptation with original levels and areas. This time, they just ported *Donkey Kong Country 2*, so it must be good?" Before I tell you that you're unfortunately wrong, I wish to define one word in your sentence, the word **port**. What is a port? Let's define it by peeling the onion of *DKL2*.

The first layer, the marketing of the game, is indeed different from the Super Nintendo game. It has a different name, uses different images to promote itself. But it is irrelevant, since a port is not defined by its appearance outside the software that makes the game. We already established previously that *Heroes of Might & Magic* on Game Boy Color was not a port simply because it reused the same name.

The second layer, once the game is played, is the world map. It is strikingly similar to the original game. The second and third areas have been merged, inside each area you have small changes here and there, and the world map is for some reason mirrored, but we do not have something that would disqualify this game as a port.

On the third layer, once you play a level, the game style and controls are nearly the same. We have a platform game with the same overall controls, with some concessions made for the four-button difference between both consoles. Gone is the team-up move, which allowed a Kong to stand on the shoulder of the other one to reach higher platforms.

It's at the fourth layer, the level layouts, that we reach the unequivocal truth that we are not playing a port, since every single level is different from the SNES game. They usually have the same theme as their SNES versions. One level is about using barrels to navigate vines, another level features jumping on reeds in a swamp. But every level is different; they're dumbed-down echoes of the SNES levels. They're meant to confuse you by looking like the Super Nintendo original levels. This highlights a fundamental truth that applies to **so many Game Boy games**: unless the original environmental resolution is maintained, a game cannot be a port. Puzzle games like *Tetris, Mario's Picross* or *Dr. Mario* require fewer pixels to function than the Game Boy has, so they can be ports. Turn-based games like *Game Boy Wars* and *Dragon Warrior I & II* can scroll and offer menus to display the same amount of data, so they can be ports (the *Game Boy Wars* games were original titles but it's just an example). Point-and-click adventure games like *Shadowgate* redraw their environments, but change nothing about their original structure so they also work. *Super Mario Bros. Deluxe* is indeed a port, since they didn't change the levels or Mario's jumping to fit within the screen. Finally, a great example is *DuckTales*. Most mentions of the Game Boy version call it a port, but it is not. It looks awfully similar to the NES game, but **a lot** has been changed in the levels to make the game possible on the portable system. This is the same with *DKL2*. Most people will call it a port, but it is definitely not a port because of the irreconcilable level differences.

So now that we've established that it is not a straight port, but a reimagining of *DKC2*, I can tell you the decisions they made to reimagine the classic SNES game are horrible. I won't go into too much detail, but suffice it to say they made an easier, shorter and way less interesting game. Levels in *DKC2* have this delicious forward momentum. You always want to unfold the next challenge. For example, in Kannon's Klaim, the second level of the second world is filled with Krocs that shoot barrels or cannonballs. You're climbing up the mine shaft, and you're constantly bombarded by new challenges using those same enemies. It's fun to discover the designers' next idea. On Game Boy, they've all been taken out. The adaptation of this level is just a repetition of Auto Fire Barrels over and over until the end of the level where you have one crocodile with a cannon. They only put one signature enemy of the level! I think they removed those enemies because they were too hard to see on the Game Boy screen, which meant they took at all the fun out of the level.

The whole game is like that. The first world on SNES, the pirate boat, is this fun, easy world with lots of secrets hidden all over the place. They took out the exploration and fun secrets on Game Boy. The third world is this swamp with interesting jumping challenges on SNES. The levels that survived the transition to Game Boy are just boring.

The most exciting section of *Donkey Kong Country 2* is Kremland, a deadly amusement park interspersed with beehives. It's this tough area with most levels featuring exciting new play styles. There are two similar roller coaster levels and they went so far has to give them two different control styles; one has the Kong jump from the cart and the other has the cart itself jump. On the other hand, the Game Boy's Kremland area is just boring. I stopped playing as I reached the Kremland area on Game Boy. I cannot believe that the developers at Rare suddenly became good at porting their own game. Their first two levels were simply too bad for me to warrant any more of my time.

Once Again Saddled With a Terrible Camera

My limited time with the game allowed me to confirm that the camera is still problematic. The game features the same twitchy camera that I hated so much with the first game. My camera experimentation also allowed me to discover another issue I have with this game. The second level of *DKC2*, Mainbrace Mayhem, is actually a personal favourite. It's set on the pirate ship's sails and I love it because you never get confused about where to go next in this vertical level that you navigate in a seesaw pattern. It does this by locking the camera's vertical scrolling; you can't make it scroll any higher by jumping when there is another section of the level above you. You can sometimes break that mechanism by jumping much higher than you normally would, but it is surprisingly effective at guiding you towards your destination without confusing you. It's not perfect, but it works surprisingly well.

DKL2 works the same way, but the level structure is more cramped, so you often jump and see level elements to the sides. You start wondering where you are supposed to go, and can easily skip whole sections of the level simply because you saw a space much later in the level you could reach. It's great if you want to quickly get through a level, but terrible in a design sense. This is a common occurrence with this game: it tries to ape the SNES game but does it in a bad way which causes confusion.

Saving & Batteries

Let's take a final moment to discuss something tangentially related to this game: batteries. My cartridge of *Donkey Kong Land 2* had a dead battery, so I had to change it. The way to know a battery is dead is your save gets deleted the second you turn off your Game Boy.

Saves on cartridge games work with a watch battery hidden inside the cartridge that keeps a small dedicated section of RAM powered without interruption for decades. If this small RAM section is without electricity, your saves are gone. It sounds crazy but it works. The battery is not getting recharged while the console is powered on either; watch batteries are non-rechargeable. It just works for decades without issues. It can stay powered on for so long because a watch battery can last a very long time if it only needs to power some small circuitry without a display.

If you buy original Game Boy cartridges in this day and age, you will eventually encounter a cartridge that no longer keeps your saves. However, if you decide to change a game's battery yourself, here are some pieces of advice:

- Buy the specific screwdriver you need to open a Game Boy cart. Do not fall for that melted pen *trick*, it's a terrible idea that always ends in a mess.

- You don't necessarily need to de-solder the battery connectors. I use a box cutter and patience to cut the very little bit of solder on the battery.

- Don't hesitate to use a slightly bigger battery. I use CR2032 batteries since they're so easy to find, and they also help with my final tip.

- Use electric tape to hold the battery snugly between

the original connectors. Since I use bigger batteries, the cartridge's plastic housing also squeezes the battery in place.

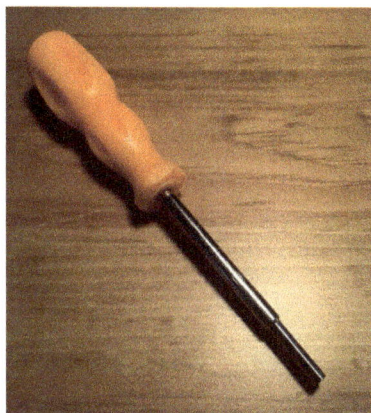

However, don't repeat my rookie mistake; don't put the battery on backward and then think the cartridge itself is broken. I had done that and was convinced my cartridge was screwed. I finally realized my mistake after an embarrassing amount of time.

Conclusion

I feel like I talked about everything around *Donkey Kong Land 2* instead of talking about this forsaken game. I did all that for good reasons, since there is not a lot to talk about. The game is slightly better than the first one, but it still is fundamentally broken. The people at Rare could have easily redesigned the core concept, but they instead just made the same mistakes again. They probably believed that adapting SNES levels and lowering the number of details in the backgrounds would be enough to improve their concept. They were wrong.

I guess it proves that the developers at Rare never lost their roots as developers of flawed games. They made interesting games before *Donkey Kong Country* when they were originally Ultimate Play the Game and afterwards as Rare. Their games usually had some sort of fatal flaw that made them impossible to love. *Battletoads* like most of their games was way too hard. *A Nightmare on Elm Street* was too complicated for its own sake. *Wizards & Warriors* had floaty controls ill-suited for the levels in the game. When they started collaborating directly with Nintendo, however, they started making flawless titles. They also severely slowed down and stopped releasing a dizzying number of games. They still had it in them to make a bunch of clunkers, it seems.

3D Pocket Pool

- European release in March 2001
- Never released in North America
- Never released in Japan
- Published by Virgin Interactive
- Developed by Aardvark Software

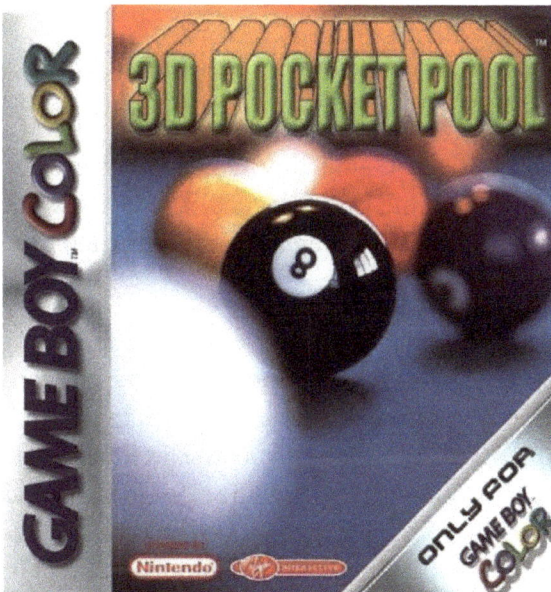

The game features a photograph for the cover but uses very stylized art in the game.

Too Late for Pool

This game feels like it's coming from another planet! *3D Pocket Pool* is this strange experience that you can't quite put your finger on. It would also be somewhat charming if not for all its problems. Let's look together at this off-kilter game, and figure out why it's essential.

Obscure Release

3D Pocket Pool was released only in Europe in 2001, during the twilight of the Game Boy Color when everybody was waiting for the Game Boy Advance. The GBA would be unleashed upon the world merely two months later.

During this era I was still playing my Game Boy Color and I missed a bunch of games because I was waiting for the GBA. So anytime I see a game from around March 2001, when Nintendo unveiled the GBA price and launch games, I can't dissociate the game from the excitement I had for the upcoming Game Boy Advance. Games like *Magi Nation*, *Oracle of Seasons* & *Oracle of Ages*, *Alone in the Dark: The New Nightmare*. Those games, and many more, saw their release overshadowed by the Game Boy Advance. And this time Europe, usually a laggard when it came to releases, was waiting at the same time as the rest of the world. Nintendo had announced the release of the Game Boy Advance in Europe a mere 11 days after North America.

3D Pocket Pool was released within this era. So what would have been an obscure release on a good day (come on, it's a pool game) was even more obscure because it was a Europe-only game for a console way past its bedtime. The developer,

British-based Aardvark Software, had clearly gone down-hill. You can find information about a reasonable amount of games they made in the '80s for British computers, but once you hit the '90s they seem to have made only two games: a port of *Duke Nukem 3D* for PlayStation in 1997 and *3D Pocket Pool* in 2001. Something is afoot. With the scope of *3D Pocket Pool*, I wouldn't be surprised if it was made by one or two people with little to no connection to Aardvark Software.

How obscure can this game be? What about this: it's the type of game that's often missing from Game Boy Color romsets. It's probably because it was not released in North America and Japan that the game is missed. More obscure than that, you're on Unseen64.

Addams Family Pool

3D is in the title; it's the reason this game exists. I doubt a top-down pool game would have been able to secure a release in 2001. However, a game with a hook could perhaps be different enough to sell. It seemingly didn't, as it never left Europe. Make no mistake: other simple games with a hook were released at that time. Simpler titles unattached to a licence that harkened back to the early years of the Game Boy were still released up to the end of 2001. *Trouballs*, *Puzzled*, and *Ultimate Surfing* are other titles from this period I could quickly find. It's not a lot, since the Game Boy Color library by then was mostly made up of licensed adaptations.

In terms of simplicity, *3D Pocket Pool* is no more compli-cated than 1990s *Side Pocket*. Outside of the whole 3D con-ceit, it's actually a simpler game. So what about that whole 3D thing? How is it possible? The game uses the exact same trick used by *Toy Story Racer*. Pre-rendered backgrounds are drawn to simulate a 3D pool table, and a sprite is used over the 3D image for each ball. A shadow effect underneath each ball is accomplished by using a flickering black sprite. The same flickering is used for the ball trajectory that appears when you line up your shot.

I kind of appreciate the gameplay because it has zero randomness. When you are lining up a shot, if the trajectory that appears shows your target going into the pocket it will always go in the pocket. It achieves this because it has no three-click system like a golf game that requires precise timing on your part. I discussed the three-click system in my *Mario Golf* article. Instead, you manually select the strength of your shot. By eliminating any sort of twitchy response from the game, it becomes a game about geometry. Can you figure out the angles required to put the balls in the pockets? However, the fun you can have when figuring out shots is severely limited by the poor simulation and camera controls. The game is also slow to operate and imposes a timer to shoot when you are playing the tournament mode. This all but ensures you will never have enough time to find a working angle.

The AI is thinking in this screenshot. You can see the thought bubbles on the top right.

Finally, the game has an AI that is extremely slow to act.

Whenever its turn comes up, it takes a long time before it shoots. You see a little thought bubble above your adversary, indicating that the character is thinking. It must be calculating a valid shot, and it takes its sweet ass time to do so. It often takes more time than you are allowed. They never even bothered showing a timer for the AI. They clearly knew their AI couldn't respond quickly, so they simply let it work without a time constraint. It means you spend more time waiting for your adversary to act than actually playing the game yourself. It kills any hope of enjoyment you could have gotten from this obscure title.

Music

How do you know a Game Boy title was developed in Europe? The noise channel is used for the melody of the music.

Funky People

The game has this tattoo parlour vibe for its cast of characters. I wouldn't be surprised to find those weird looking drawings on a trucks' mud flap. All the women characters have terribly sexist descriptions on the character select screen. You're also stuck looking at their dumb faces for the whole time you're playing. To pretend like you're playing pool with someone, they do this dumb thing where they will flip the table before your opponent plays, and change the character art above the fold to them hitting the ball. So if you pay attention and think hard about what they're trying to do, you too can figure out why they rotate the camera every time your adversary shoots the ball.

Conclusion

3D Pocket Pool is seemingly an echo of Aardvark's own 1989 game *3D Pool*. The game, released on Commodore's Amiga, billed itself as the first 3D pool game. I've watched a quick video of the Amiga game and it seems making a responsive pool game was beyond the hopes and dreams of the developers, in 1989 as well as 2001. That some people, somewhere in England, bothered to make a bad pool game for Game Boy Color in 2001 is fascinating.

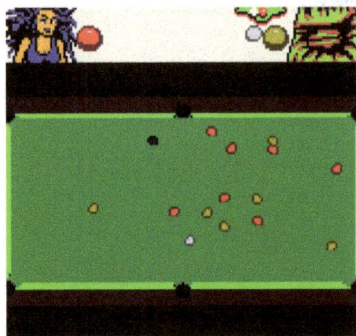

The game switches to a top-down view upon pressing Select. It just serves to show how the game is even less complex than *Side Pocket*, a game from way back in 1990.

Warlocked

- North American release in July 2000
- Never released in Japan
- Never released in Europe
- Published by Nintendo
- Developed by Bits Studios

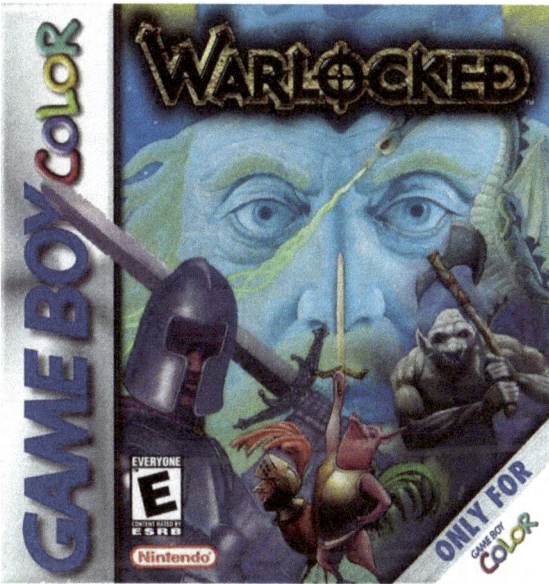

Unfortunately, I don't find the cover does this great game justice.

Portable Marvel

Warlocked is one of the reasons I started this whole project. I always wanted to talk about it. It's an impossible feat; a real-time strategy (RTS) game on Game Boy Color, filled to the brim with charm and delight. The game has so much gumption to achieve so much with so little that you will be filled with awe. *Warlocked* is the quintessential essential game.

Let's Describe the Game

Warlocked is obviously inspired by *Warcraft*'s aesthetic, but it has its own artistic merit aside from its inspiration. A game clone might have some original aesthetic, but then you load a new level and everything suddenly looks like they should be sued. *Warlocked* is not like that; it has its own style from beginning to end without falling into the pitfalls of being a clone. They copied *Warcraft*'s premise of a fantasy RTS of Orcs fighting Humans but not much else. As an example, the orcs in Blizzard's *Warcraft* live in round mud houses in a rustic world of mushrooms and green water. The orcs in *Warlocked* live in hell!

The game is a real RTS, with a top-down view and cursor controls to order your units. It has a rudimentary control scheme, a rudimentary economy, a rudimentary tactical system. You get my point. Everything is barebones, but you cannot fault the game, it's on Game Boy Color.

I have always been a perennial RTS player, so you'll forgive me if I speak gibberish when talking about the game. *Warlocked* uses the first *Warcraft* ruleset as a template. This

means it has two artistically different factions that are nonetheless identical in terms of abilities. It also means that you mine two resources: gold and wood/mountain (?) in exactly the same way *Warcraft* does it. These resources are gathered and brought back to your castle by workers. The castle is your central building that can produce more workers. In a breach of the *Warcraft* ruleset, the central castle is already built on every map you play, and cannot be rebuilt if destroyed. It's immediately Game Over. The fact this building cannot be built and is placed ahead of time is a limitation for the sake of simplicity. Think of every situation that **cannot** happen because your main building is already placed and cannot be replicated.

I'll talk about more details later on, but just keep in mind

Warlocked

that the game is legitimately an RTS. You choose your campaign, go through missions that slowly teach you the concepts and in just a moment, you're training warriors in your barracks, exploring the map, achieving objectives, defending your base, all while micromanaging your resource gathering.

Surprisingly, it brings some fresh ideas to the RTS concept. First, you have dragons, the strongest units of the game and the only flying units available. They cannot be built. Instead, you find their eggs on the map, they hatch and you bring the baby dragon back to your base. The dragon matures after a short while, and you get the dragon. It basically is capture the flag with the reward being a wonderful flying unit to smite your enemies! During single player its impact is nothing fancy, but it brings some much needed tactical complexity to multiplayer matches. Oh yes indeed, the game has multiplayer and it works perfectly well! With two cartridges, you can have a ton of fun! The second idea is related to a second multiplayer mode, based around a kind-of deck building concept. Whenever you finish a single player mission, your remaining resources are put into a pool that you can use to create armies. Those armies can then be compared against other players, using the Game Boy Color's IR port. I never was able to experience the feature since I never knew anyone who owned the game. The last idea of the game is wizards. Throughout the campaign, you will meet an assortment of unique units. They're somewhat hidden in the maps, and once they are found they join your army, and they each bring a different spell to help you. Some have passive spells, like stronger armour for all your units, while others have active spells, like turning enemy units into chickens. They all have dumb names to accompany their spell that end in -wiz, like Chickenwiz and Quakewiz. You can have a maximum of two wizards out in battle at the same time, which means you have to choose the spells you want wisely. Once you complete a mission, if the wizard survived, they join your permanent list of wizards and they can be reused in future single-player missions. It's obviously inspired by Pokémon, but be careful: if they die during a mission, they're gone for good. You can replay missions to go and get them back, however. Which means you can actually have more than one copy of each wizard. Just like Pokémon.

The best part of the whole idea is they're usable in multiplayer matches. So you can show off and use your wizards when playing against another player. I've played *Warlocked* multiplayer matches only once in my life (thanks, Mark Weissfelner). Clowning your adversary with your wizards was the most fun I had playing this game and I only managed to do it once. Drat!

WINDWIZ
This native of the
Windswept Plains

You also need to trade your wizards if you want a full set, since you cannot acquire all the different wizards with one cartridge. The trading happens over IR, just like with the armies. I have to say, this whole IR thing is bugging me.

Since the Game Boy Advance did not have this IR port, it makes it awkward to test features when you only have Game Boy Advance systems (I happen to only own one Game Boy Color at the moment). Not a fault of the game, but an unfortunate problem for me, since I'm a Game Boy Advance SP hoarder.

Learning About the Game

I have loved *Warlocked* from the word go. While all my friends had moved on from the Game Boy after the craze of the first *Pokémon* game, I stayed invested in buying and playing Game Boy titles. I had always been there, really. Between 1990 and 2001, I never stopped procuring Game Boy games. By the late '90s, I was visiting the few websites I knew who covered Game Boy releases. One website I remember is IGN, who seemed to have assigned one person to cover the Game Boy: Craig Harris. I would connect to free ISP Juno using a bugged version of its software that meant I never saw its intrusive ads (that's a hell of a story for another time), and going on IGN to see if they had any Game Boy-related news. From the first moment I heard about *Warlocked*, I knew I had to buy that game. I hoped that my local Zellers, my only source of Game Boy games, would stock the game when it was released.

IGN has slowly devolved to the point of inanity, but it still has articles from its heyday available if you use an external search engine to find them. I found two pages from 2000 mentioning *Warlocked*. Rereading those articles on IGN raises many questions about the development of the game. Why don't I ask some of the developers?

Highlighting the Workers

Looking to be original on the platform is inspiring, knowing you're breaking new ground as a developer is a key motivation, and drives you to do the hard work necessary to achieve something unique. I don't think anyone else attempted to do what we did, the game was one of its own on the platform.

— Dylan Beale, producer of *Warlocked*

I gathered enough courage to reach out to Dylan Beale, the producer of the game originally from Bits Studios, to answer some of my questions. Even though we are in the midst of a pandemic unlike anything modern society has ever seen, he found the time to patiently answer my questions. I feel so elated to have talked to the producer of one of my favourite games. He even, without me ever asking, roped in Steve Clark, the programmer of the game to answer my questions too.

I was curious about how they had the idea to make an RTS on Game Boy Color. I asked Dylan Beale how the idea for the game came about:

> Dylan: People were playing a lot of *Warcraft 2*, it was really popular amongst the staff, and naturally when you're thinking of new game ideas you can't help but be inspired by the games you're loving to play at that moment.

I'm happy Dylan didn't beat around the bush: *Warlocked* is unapologetically inspired by *Warcraft*. It has its own ideas, particularly with regards to the music and the gameplay, but the game proudly wears its inspirations on its sleeves.

Answering the same question, Steve Clark highlighted how he was convinced of working on the project by a clever technological solution.

> I first heard about the idea of doing an RTS for the Game Boy Color in a meeting with Foo Katan (the owner of Bits Studios) early in 1999. I'd gone

in to discuss potential Game Boy Color work and he mentioned the design Martin Wheeler had been working on. He had me completely hooked by an idea for how to get around the classic *sprites on a line* flicker issue when handling the sixteen by sixteen pixel sprites, which was to write them into the background map whenever they were suitably aligned.

— Steve Clark, programmer

That's how you convince people that your idea is good: you elegantly solve difficult problems for them.

The problem he's talking about his fatal to an RTS on Game Boy Color. The system cannot display more than 10 sprites on the same row across the screen. It's a hardware limitation of its display chip, there's no way around this. For those who don't know, a sprite is an element that can freely move around the screen. The enemies and characters in *Mega Man* are all made of sprites, for example, while the elements that stay solidly stuck to the background grid, like platforms and ladders, are not sprites. To further complicate things sprites are only eight by eight pixels in size on Game Boy. Most games use characters much larger than eight pixels. To make larger characters developers simply put multiple sprites next to one another to assemble characters of multiple sprites. This allows them to make characters the size they want but means the sprite limit is much tighter. In a platformer like *Super Mario Land*, you can design your levels around the limitation. You can place enemies within your levels so the player has very few chances of encountering more than the sprite limit, amongst other things. With an RTS, you're screwed. The player can move a large number of units wherever she likes. If the player wants to make a line full of workers that forces the console into an impossible display scenario, she can.

Since every unit in *Warlocked* is made of a grid of two sprites by two sprites, it would mean that you couldn't display more than five units in a row. But the game is able to display five units in a row nonetheless. How is it possible? This is where Martin Wheeler's idea comes into play. Whenever characters are immobile, they are turned into background tiles. They transform from an element that can move freely around the screen to a part of the scenery. You would not be able to see this, since there is no visual difference between a sprite and a tile. The switch from one state to the other is invisible. Your units are intrinsically connected to the background, but that's not a problem. That's exactly what you want anyway. You've ordered to stand still.

Warlocked

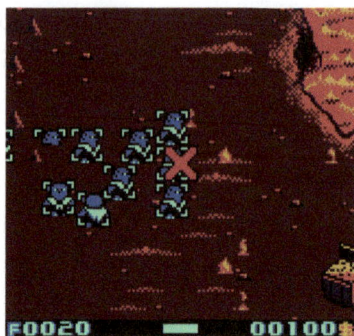

You can see that when units are moving, and are therefore not tiles, you can hit the sprite limit. Here, the limit is broken and the game stops displaying the bottom half of one unit. Other games might choose to flicker the sprites. Programmers decide exactly what happens when you reach the sprite limit.

Making a Game Boy Color title

I've often wondered how much time a Game Boy title took to make (I guesstimate at least six months), so I asked both of the guys what they experienced.

> Steve: All told the game took a little over a year from start to finish. My projects were quite varied even then, so there was no typical length as such.

> Dylan: Wow, it was a long time ago. It took longer than *R-Type DX*, but that was a port, although quite a challenging one. Creating a unique IP always requires more time, and *Warlocked* was technically challenging with its AI pathing and having many units on the screen. We would have been driven to finish by the budget, and often having a strict timeline pushes you to make creative and technical decisions, so as a function it's positive. What the budget did do was make the team work **very** hard to get it out!

Their answers are very valuable. They had budgeted for a year, and that was that, because that's what the project needed and could afford. I don't think many Game Boy Color titles would have a very different experience from theirs, since the Game Boy was well suited to straightforward development. Dylan mentioned the challenges of bringing an RTS to Game Boy, and he gave me more insights.

> Dylan: The hardest programming challenges were getting the game running speedily enough, trying to ensure the AI (whether in terms of pathfinding or defending a unit's own position) was capable enough, and, of course, multiplayer.

So Dylan mentions several specific issues that he faced while developing the game, and he then quickly went into further details for each one.

> The enemy AI was fairly simplistic, in that the units could manage to defend themselves or choose to attack, but this simplicity allowed for the game to play quickly.

I've talked about this before and I'll mention it again: the Game Boy cannot do convincing AI. It just doesn't have enough RAM and CPU speed to achieve complex enemy behaviours in real time. *Warlocked* met the same fate: as Dylan clearly says, the AI had to be simplistic for the game to exist. In fact, the enemy AI has only two behaviours:

Warlocked

- **Attacking when detecting your units:** When you move units within a certain range of enemy units, they will react by making a beeline to the unit who first made range and attack it.

- **Spawning units and heading towards your keep:** When you have been detected by specific enemy units, the pre-placed enemy barracks will start spawning units at a set rate and send them towards your keep. If they encounter one of your units or buildings, the first behaviour mentioned above will trigger. Those enemy barracks are always placed in a simple path from your keep, so the path-finding is never a problem. Speaking of pathfinding:

> The pathfinding was the single biggest issue in the whole game. There are many ways to program pathfinding, but they mostly rely on both a good amount of memory to determine the best route and a fast processor to cope with the computations. The Game Boy Color's processor simply couldn't handle some of the best algorithms for multiple units, and so a *best attempt* system was used. Although far from perfect, it does manage to navigate itself away from a number of tricky situations, and allows units to move and act as a group with some success.

Be careful, dear reader, to understand the difference between enemy AI and pathfinding. While enemy AI is the behaviour of your enemy opponent, pathfinding is the movement behaviour of all the units in the game, enemy or friendly. When you click a destination on the map, it is the constant calculation of the route to take to that destination. It's a notoriously complex computing problem, and there is no ceiling to the amount of computing power you can throw at those calculations.

Here, I have nothing but congratulations for Dylan and the rest of the team. The path-finding is constantly stumped and fails, but it does so in a very predictable manner. Units abandon when they can't find an entrance through a wall, and the path-finding is usually OK when you give your units a destination within the same screen. It's when you decide to traverse large distances or turn a sharp corner that the path-finding fails.

The game uses all sorts of tricks to alleviate potential path-finding issues like wood collecting. In a game like *Warcraft*, you have to collect wood. Workers will try to collect the wood tiles that are the closest to the lumber yard. In *Warlocked*, that was obviously too complex a behaviour to implement, so workers will simply collect wood in a straight line. It's not ideal, but again it is a predictable behaviour that you can quickly understand and control.

> Multiplayer was its own special sort of challenge, and ended up using a custom master/slave mechanism.

I can say that with the multiplayer, they succeeded. The game runs a bit slower, and the voice clips for the units are absent in this mode, but I'd dare say multiplayer is the greatest achievement of this game. A full-fledged multiplayer RTS on Game Boy Color. I own two copies of *Warlocked* just to be able to see it with my own eyes.

Warlocked

An interesting quirk is that the game completely stops whenever one of the two players goes to the wizard selection screen. It's obvious they couldn't run both the selection screen and the game at the same time.

The Control Scheme

When I asked Dylan about the challenges the game encountered, he mentioned the interface:

> From the graphics and interface side, squeezing the control system into something that used just two to four buttons and the D-Pad was something that gave me a lot of pride. Without being too fiddly, it's possible for the player to perform a vast array of actions without having to resort to cumbersome text menus, which would break the flow of the game.

Let's quickly address the game's user interface. The game has a small black status bar at the bottom of the screen which has all the typical RTS information. Wood/Mountain and Gold amount are always present near the corners, and the middle of the bar features contextual information. The manual is pretty clear about the status bar's functionalities.

The game's controls are fascinating. The game manages to squeeze all the barebones RTS controls into a D-Pad and

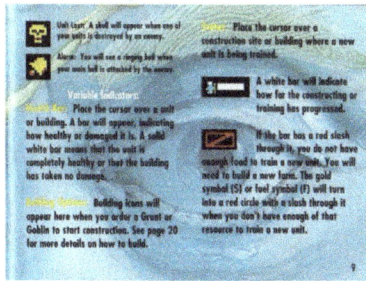

four buttons. It even manages to have some surprising features: guarding another unit, ordering the construction of buildings, and even unit control groups.

The controls start and end with the cursor. Managing to move it is unfortunately the clunkiest part of the interface; a mouse is much better for this purpose, but all we have is the D-Pad. You eventually learn to get by, particularly if you learn to hold the B button to speed up your cursor speed.

When you have no units selected, the cursor is a big hand. Whenever you hover over a unit, you can select it using the A button. Once you have selected the unit, you can order it on the map using the A button again. Holding the A button releases your selected unit, freeing you to select another one.

To train units, you simply bring the cursor over the building you wish to use, and you press A to start training. It's easy as that. But wait a minute! There are two units that can be trained in the barracks: the warrior and the archer. How do you train two units with one button? You press A for a warrior, B for an archer when your cursor is over a barracks. They didn't even need to implement a menu.

That's the minimum amount of control systems you need for an RTS. *Dune 2*, the first significant RTS, has no functionality beyond that in terms of unit and building control. And in that game, you needed to select the movement action on the keyboard before performing it. Every time.

Warlocked thankfully goes beyond the bare minimum. Instead of pressing the A button, if you hold it with no units selected, you can select multiple units by drawing a rectangle with the cursor. It's now a given that an RTS will allow you to select multiple units, so you might be surprised that I'm considering this above the bare minimum, but that shit had to be invented. Like I said previously, *Dune 2* allowed only a single unit to be selected at once.

However, the unit selection comes with some caveats. There is no visual cue surrounding your box; it's literally invisible. You also have a limited selection range. You cannot make a box larger than four units by four. This can be vexing; you can easily have fewer than 16 units, but spread over a much larger area than a perfect square four units wide. This makes it tiring to have to move each unit separately to fit within the small unit selection box. One thing that would help is a way to assign a control group, and surprise surprise, *Warlocked* can assign two control groups! This game has a feature that *Warcraft II* didn't have at launch! Since you only have two buttons, and they're already accounted for, what button are you meant to use? Select, of course. Pressing Select and holding the A or B button creates a group with your currently selected units. Afterwards, pressing Select will reselect your last control group, and Select with a quick press of A or B will highlight that group for you. I have to admit I never used the feature when I initially got the game as a teenager; the part where you have to hold Select to create a group always stumped me. Instead, I made units guard others in my army. That way all of my army could move together when I moved the units being guarded. It was clunkier, but that's all I could figure out how to use.

The final order of business in the game is the worker. How do you build structures when all the buttons are so overloaded with functionality? The game reuses the B button and it works OK. Whenever you have workers selected, the game will display a construction overlay on the ground automatically. Pressing the B button will present a small menu in the status bar, where you can choose which building to build with the D-Pad.

Once that's done, you're good to go; your workers will take care of the rest.

The Music!

I implore you to listen to the soundtrack of *Warlocked*. The soundtrack is made by a composer known for his Commodore 64 work, Jeroen Tel, and it has that wonderful *European composer* quality that is so powerful on Game Boy. It has this interesting emotional undercurrent that really elevates the whole game. My favourite tracks are *Lava 1* and *Woods 1*. I think I get this feeling because the game is trying something different from the usual understated Game Boy music. RTS music tends to be very preeminent; there's a strong tradition in the genre of the music never taking a step back during gameplay. I guess we have Frank Klepacki, composer of Westwood titles, to thank for his active soundtracks. *Warlocked does* the same thing. It has an energetic soundtrack that draws attention to itself, by taking inspiration from *Warcraft 2: Tides of Darkness*. The soundtrack in that game is unforgettable and grabs your attention immediately. *Warlocked* goes for the same effect and **I love it.**

When I first bought the game as a teenager in 2000, I would start the music test on a track I liked, connect headphones to my Game Boy Color, put it in my pockets and walk to school listening to the music. I liked it that much.

Conclusion

I have to thank Dylan Beale and Steve Clark for their insights into the game. I did not feature every single quote they gave me in this article, but I learned a lot from their openness. They're the first Game Boy developers I talked to, and I could never have hoped for a better duo. Thank you guys.

I guess I also have to thank them for making *Warlocked*! This game is such a wonderful curiosity, and it couldn't have happened without all the developers' sheer force of will. They made an RTS on Game Boy Color. And it's not bad, far from it. You owe it to yourself to play it, it's essential. Those guys shot for the moon and they actually succeeded!

Kid Icarus: Of Myth and Monsters

- North American release in November 1991
- European release in May 1992
- Never released in Japan
- Published by Nintendo
- Developed by Nintendo & TOSE

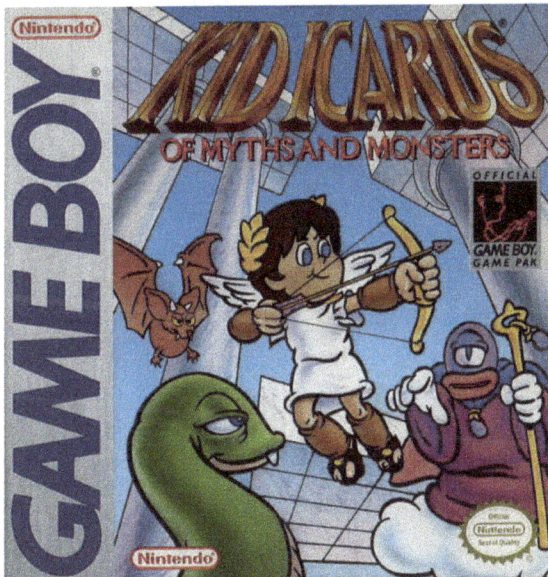

They don't make them like they used to.

Not Kidding

Kid Icarus: Of Myth and Monsters can be a frustrating game. Bear in mind, playing it is not particularly frustrating. I'd argue Nintendo, collectively as a company, is the best video game developer stable in the world, so very few of their games are wholly frustrating. They have a strong company culture that focuses on exactly the right things. But games like *Kid Icarus: Of Myth and Monsters* are expertly made but lack any valuable contributions, and that's why I'm frustrated. The choices the game makes are pedestrian; you're left with a bittersweet taste after completing it, never reaching the greatness you hoped for. Even though it is expertly made by Nintendo with support from the shadowy TOSE.

Perhaps this development structure, of a Nintendo employee taking care of the design with TOSE delivering the programming under contract is why I feel underwhelmed. *Metroid II: Return of Samus* was also designed by the same person, Masafumi Sakashita, and I love that game. However, *Metroid II* was fully designed and programmed by Nintendo R&D1 developers with no outside work-for-hire. With both games designed at the same time *Metroid II* was clearly the primary project since they made it internally. This Game Boy sequel of *Kid Icarus* ends up a lesser work made with far less precious developer time. Let's explore further the situations surrounding this lesser, but still essential, work.

An Angel in Context

For release in the fall of 1991, Nintendo R&D1 had two games under development that ended up released. *Metroid II: Return of Samus* was developed internally while they tasked

Masafumi Sakashita *Kid Icarus: Of Myth and Monsters* with support from TOSE's developers. Those games are interesting for how they are both different compared to R&D1's previous Game Boy titles. After the initial games released with the Game Boy in the middle of 1989, the developers at Nintendo R&D1 made and released *Dr. Mario, Radar Mission* and *F-1 Race* in 1990. Those games clearly continue in the same vein as the earliest Game Boy titles made by R&D1. They are simpler pick-up and play titles without any save features that can be enjoyed during quick gaming sessions. By contrast, *Metroid II* and this second *Kid Icarus* game are both involved exploration games with a save function. To me, this reads as a pivot for the creators of the Game Boy. Before 1991 they developed and released tailor-made experiences for a portable console. They made a new puzzle game starring Mario (that they also released on NES), they made their take on the board game *Battleship*, and they made a small racing game showcasing a new four-player peripheral.

With their two 1991 games they were instead making faithful sequels to games that were made for NES but adapted for a portable context. Moving forward this would be the new normal on Game Boy. Case in point, 1990 was the year with the most puzzle game releases. Games moving forward would be more *lounging on the couch waiting for dinner* and less *sitting in the bus waiting for your stop*. In a sense this is Nintendo catching up to some prescient third-party developers who had already figured out how to make more involved games, with titles like *Double Dragon*, *Ghostbusters 2*, and *Final Fantasy Legend*.

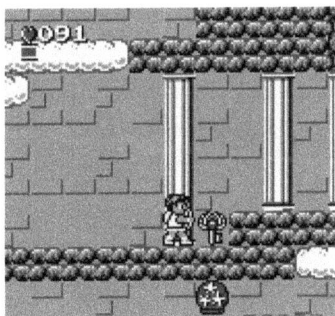

Interestingly, Nintendo R&D1 would never again develop more than one Game Boy title a year after 1991. I believe their reduced output is due to their work on the Virtual Boy at the time. We know that by 1991, Gunpei Yokoi and the rest of R&D1 were already working on the Virtual Boy. Keep in mind, counting the cancelled games we are aware of, Nintendo R&D1 developers worked on at least ten games for the failed successor to the Game Boy. That's enough to occupy a division for five years for sure. Adding on top of that the long, protracted, and complicated development on the Virtual Boy itself, it's no wonder Gunpei Yokoi and his team had little time to spare to develop Game Boy titles between 1991 and 1995. I can't shake the feeling playing *Kid Icarus: Of Myth and Monsters* that I'm playing a game that R&D1 made as a side project.

Another interesting aspect of the release of this *Kid Icarus* is its North American exclusivity. The game never saw a Japanese release. With 1990's *Balloon Kid* also never released in Japan, 1992's *Wave Race* doing the same again, and *Metroid II* releasing in North America months before hitting Japan, it seems Nintendo was somehow uninterested in its own home market. This is a bit of a mystery to me. The hardware sales do not support Nintendo losing interest in the Japanese Game Boy market: their numbers were strong. I've previously talked about a similar situation happening after 1998, where Nintendo released games in the US and Europe that were never released in Japan, but around 2000 the Game Boy Color hardware was selling four times faster outside Japan. This big discrepancy explains why their focus was on their growing markets between 1999 and 2001. In 1991, however, the Game Boy had similar hardware sales numbers around the world, so I don't have an easy answer as to why Japan saw so few releases from Nintendo themselves for two years. Maybe I'm missing something?

An Angel on Your TV

Let's talk about the original Famicom/NES *Kid Icarus*. I had yet to really play the original *Kid Icarus* before I decided to write this article. It's a bit shocking to be honest, how hard they made the game starring the little angel with a naked butt in Valentine's Day cards. Why is the game so hard? *Kid Icarus*'s controls are difficult to master, and all its mechanics are half-baked. Let's discuss those sins.

The biggest one is the spawning enemies that populate the levels. Instead of each enemy being placed by the designer of the game, as in *Super Mario Bros.*, the game simply assigns an enemy wave to discrete level segments. When the screen is scrolled within that segment, the game will always spawn the same enemy wave again and again until you scroll to the next segment. Then it will start to spawn the enemy waves that corresponds to that new segment. It makes the game more difficult because you're always stuck facing enemies without getting a break, but more than that it's just boring. There's no intelligent enemy placement, it's just wave after wave of the same enemies coming from the same directions, doing the same things over and over again. You don't experience the artistry of a deviously placed Goomba thwarting your plans.

Another issue is hammers. Throughout the game, you're slowly gathering them. They're hard to find, since they're acquired through a two-step process, and feel precious. What do you ultimately gain with this precious resource? They give you shitty one-shot mooks during boss fights. Boo-urns.

Another thing: Let's say you manage to survive one of

these really tough gauntlets, that are also criminally boring, and you are rewarded with an upgrade. However, the game requires you to have a minimum level of life for the treasure to unlock and be usable. Don't get confused, it's not like the Master sword in *The Legend of Zelda* that shoots only when at full health; you only need to hit the health threshold once to permanently unlock the upgrade. Why did they implement it that way? There's no need for it, no reason.

The Game Boy sequel unfortunately features the same boring gauntlets to receive the upgrades.

Oh and one last thing; any acquired upgrade is temporarily removed when you are in a dungeon. No increased arrow range, no defensive crystals, no nothing during the three longest game sections. Why? I think they realized the dungeons were too easy with the upgrades so they took them away. Whatever the reason for this decision, it's just mean.

An Angel in Your Hands

There's a lot less egregious stuff in *Kid Icarus: Of Myth and Monsters*. They fixed many things to make the game enjoyable.

- The controls are much improved, with jumps being much more adjustable. The game also introduces a sloweddown descent (with Kid Icarus flapping his small wings) when you mash the A button.

- You don't die when you touch the bottom of the screen; the game simply scrolls in all four directions.
- Your upgrades work under the same system as in *The Legend of Zelda*; they work only when you are above a certain health level, making the game more fun since you have to thread carefully.
- Hammers are used to acquire all sorts of stuff, making them useful to collect.
- The game features a save function instead of a password system.
- The text encountered in each room is in coherent English.
- The game is much easier.

And best of all, enemies don't haphazardly spawn without any artistry. Most enemies still spawn, but they spawn at a far slower pace, giving you more time to react and prepare for their attacks. They do so in a much more thoughtful manner, spawning in far smaller sections that feel much better arranged with the level layouts. This enhances the challenges you're facing.

All these small improvements highlight the important thing about *Kid Icarus: Of Myth and Monsters*. It is a small-scale sequel without any big change to the original game's formula. The game still has the same number of levels, the exact same structure, the same collectable upgrades, the same way to collect those upgrades. It's commendable that they were able to adequately design the game to be brought forward to the Game Boy, but outside of this good work of translating the design of the game for a portable system while designing a sequel, the game has no inventive idea. It's just a sequel. Let's compare it once again to *Metroid II*, which decided to bring forward the premise and gameplay of the first game, but focused the whole game on the devious idea that

Samus Aran was hunting down Metroids to eradicate the species. They implemented new concepts to go with their premise, with a counter to indicate how many are left to kill, the creatures transforming before your very eyes, and fun twists on the game's formula during the game's last act.

Conclusion

On Game Boy Essentials, I have tried again and again and again and again to stop people from considering a Game Boy version *just a port* of a game. The resolution, limited colours and portable nature of the Game Boy made it difficult to simply port a title to the console. The overwhelming majority of Game Boy games usually called ports are not, since they make fundamental changes to the original game. *Kid Icarus: Of Myth and Monsters* is no different, but boy oh boy does it make my job more difficult. An undiscerning person might quickly conclude that both games are but two sides of the same coin. Don't make that mistake. Just play the game and see how an attentive developer with a good subcontractor can make a reasonably good game out of what was already an old-fashioned Famicom title by 1991.

Let's give a final shootout to TOSE, the chameleon of game development; they'll adapt to whatever is required, always staying invisible. In this case I don't think they are at fault for the slight problems of *Kid Icarus: Of Myth and Monsters*. The people at Nintendo wanted two sprawling games for the Game Boy in 1991 that would particularly please the North American market. It's just that this game was far less important than *Metroid II: Return of Samus*. TOSE simply provided what was asked of them. They once again played the role of the chameleon.

For my next article, I want to talk about *Wave Race*, Shigeru Miyamoto's first foray into Game Boy development that happened the year after this game got released. That game started

Miyamoto's EAD division also releasing around one title a year for Game Boy.

Damn eggplant wizards.

Wave Race

- Released in North America in July 1992
- Released in Europe in June 1997
- Never released in Japan
- Published by Nintendo
- Developed by Pax Softnica & Nintendo EAD

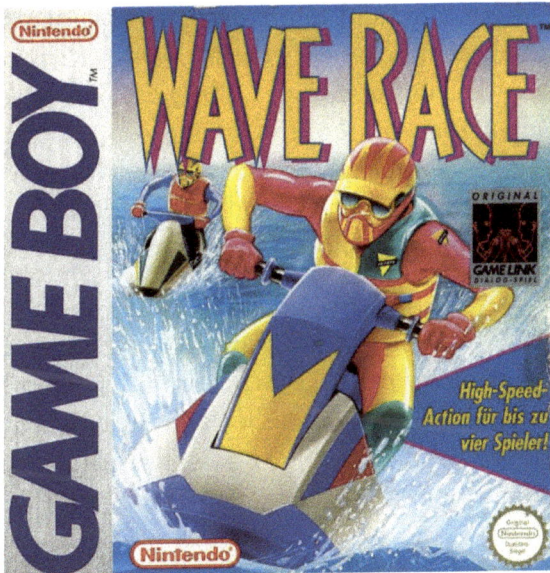

The neon colours and faux 3D screams early 90s.
Radical, dude!

The Wunderkind Is Here

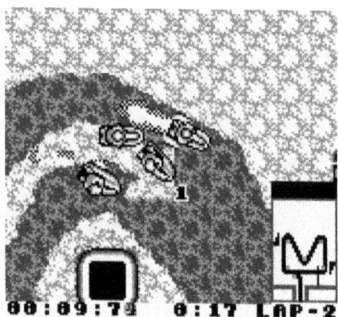

In 1992, Shigeru Miyamoto made his first Game Boy game with *Wave Race*. This is important, not because *Wave Race* is this extraordinary game; it's actually quite ordinary. It's important because it's the only time Miyamoto joined a party late. Outside of *Wave Race*, Miyamoto has been front and centre on day one with a marquee title that helps define a new system (*Donkey Kong* on Famicom, *Super Mario World*, *Super Mario 64*, *Super Mario Advance*, *Luigi's Mansion*). For the other exception, the Virtual Boy, he stayed completely away from that console and so never joined the party at all, and he described the Virtual Boy as a toy, not a console.

With *Wave Race*, Miyamoto was riding in the wake of other developers instead of making the waves himself. It is a unique opportunity to see how Miyamoto works when he's not directly collaborating with the hardware designers during the development of a console. That undeniably makes *Wave Race* essential.

Conjecture

Why did Miyamoto start designing games for the Game Boy so late? We have no exact idea, but looking at where the Game Boy stood around 1992, we can mount a reasonable theory. With Yokoi's R&D1 hard at work on project VR32, which will ultimately become the Vir-

tual Boy, their output on Game Boy was reduced to one game a year. Hiroshi Yamauchi, Nintendo's fearless CEO, probably decided that this was not enough games to sustain the momentum of their most successful system. Miyamoto was then asked to develop games for it, with a third-party company assigned to work with him: Pax Softnica. This is the same structure that was used for the development of *Kid Icarus: Of Myths and Monsters*, with one Nintendo employee, Masafumi Sakashita, supported by employees from a contracted company. Does Miyamoto's collaborative effort compare favourably to Sakashita's efforts? Yes, but both games do vastly different things.

Retrogaming in 1992

The most important difference between *Kid Icarus* and *Wave Race* is that Miyamoto made a backwards-looking title. The most interesting 1992 Game Boy titles are more involved experiences than this jet ski racing game. It feels more like a 1990 Game Boy title. I would have expected something with far more configurability, or with a great personality. *Super Mario Kart*, in a sense. Instead, the game is limited in a way that makes me feel like Miyamoto was aping R&D1's style. At first glance, *Wave Race* looks like a different interpretation of *F1 Race*, the inaugural four-player adapter title. You don't see any charming interactions, with the game sticking close to its subject matter. The game has a save feature, but only to keep track of your time records and to tell which engine class championships you have unlocked. With the championships forcing you to redo all the races of the previous classes, this makes the game more repetitive than it ought to. Think about it, this means that whatever selection you make, you will always have to start with the same race. It's as if a Mario Kart championship always started with the same exact race. There are two types of circuits, however, which greatly helps to shake things up. You have a racing circuit, but also a point-chasing game, where you have to go through gates to gather points. The caveat is that each gate only gives point to the first player to go through. This means you have to chase different routes than your adversaries. It's neat, and I'm wondering if this is a racing style that exists in real life.

All in all, the game is simple, but there is that element of Miyamoto magic present, this tireless focus on core gameplay that I love so much about him.

The Miyamoto Touch

I've previously discussed racing games with other perspectives, but this is our first top-down racing game. *Wave Race* uses a top-down perspective with directional, instead of *tank*, controls. It's very well done, with everything you need to help you succeed despite the limited point of view and constant scrolling action. You have a map with dots for the racers, helpful ranking numbers right next to your character so you don't have to spend a moment looking away from the centre of the screen. It's a busy game for the slow screen of the original Game Boy, but it does not become impossible to see; you can always see what's happening. It does that by using very clean, repeating patterns for the water you race on. Even though things are blurry, the repeating pattern helps your brain make sense of the blur.

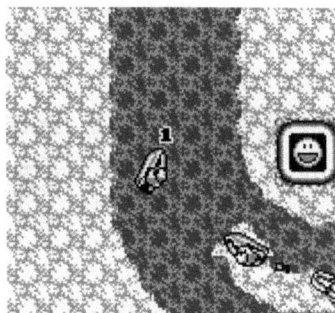

Racing on water means you can't brake; the game uses this

simple fact as the core gameplay hook of the whole game. Can you manage tight turns without brakes? The manual informs you that the best turning method is to let go of the gas as you enter the turn, use momentum to rotate your vehicle and then hit the boost right as you exit the turn to sharpen your angle. It's fun to do. You also have to be careful to make sure you have enough boosting power for each turn, since it regenerates very slowly.

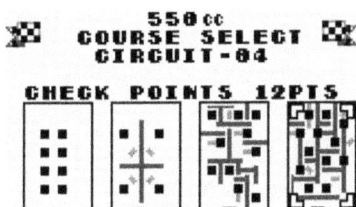

I like the conceit of the slowly regenerating boost. It starts every race empty, and you really have to manage it. I think it's there because your throttle is digital, and that meant that there's no way to represent a rev-up during a turn to push your jet ski closer to the turn. By using a boost that you hit with the second button, you can mimic this precise throttling action. For a game with such a heavy focus on precise arcade-style racing, power-ups would be an unconventional addition. Surprisingly, the game has two special items, represented by animals, that give you a temporary special power. But those upgrades, coupled with the funky hazards peppered throughout the race, are to me an expression of Miyamoto's design philosophy. They make the game interesting at all times. You are never simply running in a direction, doing nothing but pressing a button. You are constantly distracted, pushed and pulled in different directions. It's never boring.

The final element that keeps the game exciting at all times is the AI. It is reasonably good. They ram you when you get

Wave Race

too close, they step in front of you to deny passage, they steal the special items, and they pull ahead of you and do not wait around if you make too many mistakes. I know they're controlled by very simple logic, but time and effort were clearly spent to make them interesting. I can clearly see that Miyamoto sweat over their reactions.

Conclusion

Until the reorganization of Nintendo divisions in 2003, Miyamoto was in the trenches developing games through the management of his own division, Nintendo EAD. Sweating over AI racers in Game Boy games. After 2003, Miyamoto took a gradual step away from managing a team, and he became this kind of internal consultant, able to provide input to his cadre of protégés who are themselves responsible for the overall management of all of Nintendo's teams. This has made him the most senior artisan in the company, supporting every single project at the company with his insights. When Nintendo CEO Satoru Iwata suddenly died in 2015, Miyamoto even rose to the position of interim co-CEO with Genyo Takeda during the search for a replacement. The father of Mario oversaw the whole gosh darn company for years. Miyamoto is without any doubt the person with the largest impact on the company.

With *Wave Race*, we have this artifact from a time where Nintendo's most important executive wasn't supervising the whole company's output, and instead had to design a small game for a console he didn't help to create. What an interesting legacy for such a low-key game.

Sold in the United Kingdom, this set included a Game Boy Pocket and two games, *Wave Race* and *Metroid II: Return of Samus*.

Dragon Warrior III

- Japanese release in December 2000
- North American release in July 2001
- Never released in Europe
- Published by Enix
- Developed by Enix & TOSE

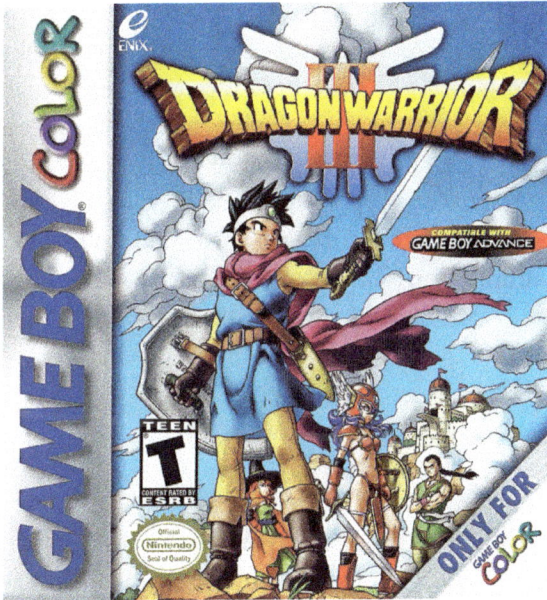

Pure adventure.

The video game discussed here was created in part by composer Sugiyama Koichi, who has publicly and financially supported historical negationism of Japanese war atrocities for decades. His vile activism should never be forgotten.

The Classiest of the Classiest

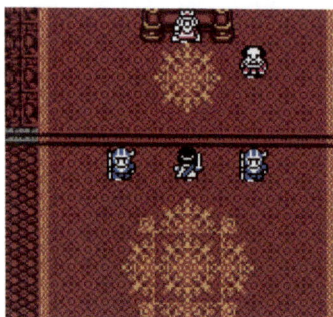

I love *Dragon Warrior III* (*Dragon Quest III* nowadays and in Japan upon its release). It's a cozy pair of slippers for my soul. When I'm mentally exhausted at the end of the day, I simply sit down, put my legs up and enjoy playing this magnificent video game. I then relax by slowly un-wrapping the game, step by step, battle by battle, dungeon by dungeon, town by town. It's never too complicated or diffi-cult, meaning I don't have to concentrate too hard to progress and a fatal mistake only costs half your gold. Join me, why won't you, on this essential quest to talk about my love for *Dragon Warrior 3* for Game Boy Color.

Colours?

I want to start by talking about colours. Yes, colours. I've heard from many people that the Game Boy Color's palette is ugly, with its muted and dull colours. I don't think they are particularly unpleasant but I do agree that on an original system, with its unlit display, the colours tend to wash out. Developers clearly dealt with this problem in their own way, giving lieu to a lot of games with strange choices. *Dragon Warrior III*'s colour choices make me feel all warm inside. I love the beautiful pairing of red and gold for the ubiqui-tous castle carpets. It has a very regal look that makes you feel comfortable. Whenever you stop to look at a single tile making up a wall or a roof, you can find small intricate details that would normally go unnoticed. It's incredible the amount of effort that went into every corner of this game. Travelling through this chibi fantasy world is a wonderful experience. There's always more to explore in every new town, a different corner of the map to unveil, an unseen enemy type to encounter. One reason the game is so beautiful is Toriyama Akira's art style is perfect for a low resolution. Famously known as the creator of *Dragon Ball*, Toriyama Akira has always been the dedicated character and creatures designer of the series. Whenever you compare his initial enemy drawings with the final result adapted for the pixellated screen of old systems, the number of retained details is impressive.

After the art is redrawn with such graphical constraints, you get to appreciate what makes his art style thrive here. His use of big eyes and in general large facial features while keeping a low line count is what impresses me the most. He obviously knew he was working within specific constraints and drew unique creatures that would work well with small sprites and limited colour choices. Look at his drawing of the golem, made for the first *Dragon Quest* game.

It has an aggressive pose, menacingly moving towards you. It looks like a cell from an animated film. Compare that with Amano Yoshitaka's golem from the first *Final Fantasy*.

It's not as simple, not as iconic. You won't find this drawing on a shirt. To be fair, I don't think Yoshitaka had the same intention; he seems focused on making menacing monsters, readability be damned. The complicated relationship between Yoshitaka and the pixel artist for Square, Shibuya Kazuko (she often made pixel art of characters before the drawings were even made), doesn't help consistency either. Which reinforces my point that Toriyama's art style and methods are better suited to the Famicom's limitations.

I'm talking about the Famicom here because the game was originally released on that system in February 1988. Subsequently released in the US on NES in March 1992, the game is what elevated the series to its revered status in Japan. It has a four-character party, with custom-built characters and an interesting list of job options, a simple class system, and a massive world to explore. For its time, it was a tour de force that such a complicated set of features was offered in an accessible package. Other RPGs of the era were often mean with their difficulty and obtuse with their explanations. The *Dragon Quest* games succeeded because they took pride in providing a game that was never punishing; failing at the game only ever meant losing half your gold and being transported back to your last save location. You never lose your hard-earned experience points and you're never forced to reload a save. Because of its ease of use and lack of punishment, it's a perfect RPG for an old curmudgeon like me who feels an urge to foolishly stay stuck in the past.

A Super Famicom Game in Your Pocket

The game was brought to Game Boy Color in 2001, but it wasn't the first time the game was remade for another system. In 1993, the company Heart Beat entered the fray as the new supporting developers of Dragon Quest titles, starting with a remake of *Dragon Quest III* on Super Famicom. To understand the importance of that detail, we need to step back and look at the development history of the series. The Dragon Quest games have a unique development structure; the trio of Horii Yuji, Toriyama Akira, and Sugiyama Koichi are responsible for their specific tasks, but the brunt of the development is done by a contracted company, initially Chunsoft. Enix (now Square Enix) ultimately publishes the games in Japan. By the time the Super Famicom became the home of the series, Chunsoft's titles were underwhelming in many ways. The graphics were dated but more than that the user interface and speed of the games felt stuck in the past; they felt like old Famicom games. Their titles sold well, and *Dragon Quest V* is widely regarded as a masterpiece, but it's clear that the trio of Yuji, Akira and Koichi wanted something better. So Chunsoft was given the boot, and Heart Beat took over their role as the company developing the games. *Dragon Quest III* on Super Famicom is the first title made by this team of developers, and I think they blew it out of the park. They lavished a ton of effort and cut no corner. Their most impressive work is undoubtedly the full attack animations for every single enemy of the game.

It's exquisite work, seemingly drawn by a team of artists at ArtePiazza. Heart Beat introduced new dungeons to explore once you have beaten the game, along with a fun new class, the Thief, and other less successful gameplay additions we'll broach later. It's a masterclass in how to improve on a previously released title, and the crazy thing with the 2001 release on Game Boy Color is that every element of the Super Famicom game was brought over to the portable title, even the intricate enemy attack animations. Those animations are beautiful on Super Famicom, but they're a notch above on Game Boy Color for the mere fact that they're there. They took the time to redraw each and everyone of them for this Game Boy Color port.

I can think of no other GBC game with such smooth animation. We have TOSE, the shadowy developer, to thank for this Game Boy Color *tour de force*. It must have been a monumental job to redraw so many things to fit within the colour constraints of the diminutive console, and to bring over all those animations.

My Personal Connection

I didn't know about any of those details when I bought the game. What had convinced me to buy it was the poster for Nintendo Power 144, one of the first issues I read when I first subscribed to the magazine. I wanted to learn more about the upcoming Game Boy Advance and my English-reading abilities were now good enough to read a game magazine by then. The poster features the cover art for the box and cartridge, a beautiful Toriyama Akira drawing, but what ultimately drew me in were all the details about the game on the back of the poster.

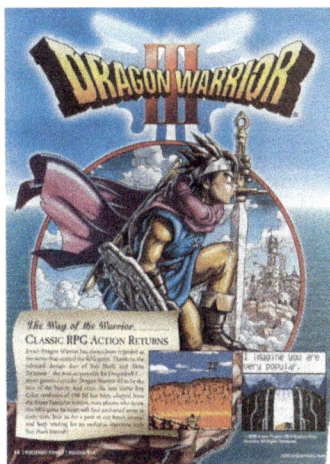

It's nothing more than an ad in the form of a daily journal, but I was hooked and wanted to buy the game, even though the Game Boy Advance was out by this point and I could have spent my hard-earned money on more impressive games. However, there was a problem. The only store near me that sold games, my local Zellers, did not have the game when I went there following its July release. Perhaps the Sears catalogue would carry it come the Christmas season; with the Game Boy Advance now released, I knew this was a long shot. My only chance to buy the game was seemingly gone.

But by 2001, a new online store had opened, available for any resourceful 15-year old. I borrowed my parent's credit card after much pleading, and I ordered from a new website, recently available in Canada, offering an incredible selection of merchandise and affordable shipping: amazon.ca. I do not have my order in my account anymore (I changed my Amazon account in 2004 for some reason), but *Dragon Warrior III* was my first online purchase, way back in the prehistoric era of 2001. I still remember going to my neighbourhood's community mailbox, and the excitement I felt at finally seeing the packages key in our family's little mailbox. Opening the package was exhilarating. A delivery from the internet. How unique! I immediately enjoyed its opening (particularly the battle between Ortega and the dragon, which feels like a Dragon Ball combat sequence), its previously mentioned colour palette, and the blazing fast walking speed. Oh man that walking speed is so sweet. You just zip through every screen at what feels like the speed of light, and I feel so grateful to the developers of the Super Famicom reissue for doing that, and for TOSE for bringing it to their Game Boy Color version. The developers valued your time, and don't want you to waste any time uselessly. I begrudge any RPG without a quick walking speed because of this specific game.

Once I had built a party, an interesting prospect since you're forced to make heartbreaking class choices, you start exploring the world and discover the previously mentioned enemy animations, and the day and night cycle. It feels like nothing special, but the fact that TOSE managed to keep the Game Boy screen readable while conveying nighttime is a small feat in itself. Unfortunately, the second world map you explore much later is always in nighttime, and that's a bummer. You don't get to enjoy the beautiful day palette.

The game is great but not everything added with the Super Famicom reissue is perfect. I particularly take umbrage at the personality system. The initial test for your hero character's personality is fun (particularly the unique final scenario to evaluate your reactions to a specific situation), but personalities' numerical impact is never explained. Here's the down-low: each personality impacts stat growth at level-up in positive or negative ways. You can gather books throughout the game to change your character's personalities, but I would have preferred if the game was clear about what each personality did, especially since they are not equal. Two or three specific personalities are clearly better out of a large set of mostly inconsequential stuff. As it stands, nothing tells you if the personalities you find are improvements from what you have.

They also added Tiny Medals, unique hidden collectibles you can find and trade for increasingly better rewards. Since there is no way to precisely track which medal you already found, it can quickly become tedious to retrace your steps to look for medals you might have missed. Fortunately, you don't need every single medal to get all the rewards, and the Thief class has two spells to alleviate your quest for the JRPG equivalent of loose change hidden between the sofa cushions.

Not Hard

Dragon Quest games have never been hard; since the very first title the consequence for dying is merely losing half your money and being sent back to your last save location. Another gameplay element has defined the series: Magic Points are only restored by staying at an inn except for some rare exceptions. These two core concepts make the series favour attrition over any other sort of challenge. It's about your party's ability to reach the end of the dungeon before they run out of magic points, not about the particular challenge of each battle. This makes the adventure soothing and fun for me. I like playing a game to see how deep inside a cavern you can go all while searching for treasure. Not every game needs to be a tense gauntlet like *Dark Souls*.

So *Dragon Quest III* is really fun to passively explore as a kind of way to keep your hands busy while you relax. As a big bonus to the exploration fun the world map is patterned after the real world; you start on an island that doesn't exist but then you get teleported to fake Italy and go from there. That way it's always fun to figure out where you are compared to the real world, and what hall of mirrors parody of a nation you'll encounter next.

Once you enter a dungeon though you're on your own. The game only offers a world map; you get no such luxury anywhere else. This could be a big turn off for many people, and I completely agree if you don't want to play an RPG that doesn't have dungeon maps, especially if it has the small viewable area of the Game Boy Color. However, the absence of a map is not always a nonstarter; great developers will adapt their design to present a cohesive map that players can learn. *Dragon Quest III*, for the most part, offers simple dungeons that won't be too hard to understand. Since you won't have the crutch of a map to rely on you'll also learn and retain the structures of the game. After twenty years of playing, I instinctively know all the towers and caverns of the game *because* there isn't a map.

Conclusion

I'll still be playing *Dragon Quest III* when I'm 80 years old, and I'll play it on Game Boy Color like god intended. The mobile versions have terrible redrawn sprites and all sorts of poor artistic choices. Please do me a favour and stay away. I also cannot wrap my head around playing that game tethered to a television. I want to put on a podcast and relax in my sunroom with the game in my hands, the dog at my feet, and my wife next to me. That's my definition of heaven.

Pokémon: Red, Green & Blue

- Japanese release in February 1996 of Red & Green and October 1996 of Blue (exclusive to CoroCoro Comic)
- North American release in September 1998 based on Japanese Blue
- European release in October 1999
- Published by Nintendo
- Developed by Game Freak

Green Version?

A Game Boy Resurrection

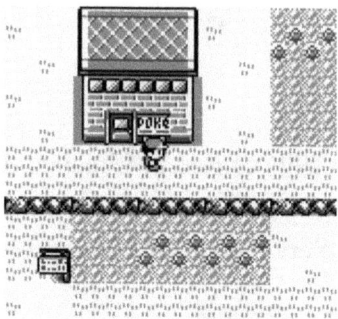

Before it became a perennial staple of popular culture with its card games and anime series and yearly releases, *Pokémon* was a world filled with mysteries. Friends would trade Pokémon monsters using the Link Cable but they would also trade legends, tall tales of dubious veracity, secret incantations of duplications, and methods to find strange and forbidden monsters.

That's why, dear reader, I invite you to follow me starting on Route 1 throughout Kanto as I unveil the answer to the following mysteries:

- What Secret Game Probably Inspired Pokémon's Creator?
- What Did Game Freak Publish Before Making Video Games?
- Which Surprising Pokémon Was Born First?
- What Horrible NES Game Funded the Development of Pokémon?
- Who Really Owns the Pokémon Franchise?
- Why Does the Game Have a Green Version in Japan?
- Why Did It Take Two Years for the Game to Be Localized and Released in North America?
- How Did Pokémon Teach Me About the Idiosyncratic Québec Media Landscape?
- Are There More Than 150 Pokémon?
- Is the Game Any Good?

Well, maybe that mystery about the amount of Pokémon

is a bit dated, considering there are now [he looks at Bulbapedia] 901 Pokémon, and that's without counting all those variants and gigantic versions of all the old ones. I even heard there are some Pokémon amongst the newer ones that aren't well designed! Gasp!

Let's forget all about those newer creations and go back to a time when everybody was wondering if there would ever be another game and Pikablu had not yet captured our imaginations.

What secret game probably inspired Pokémon's creator?

First let's go back to 1989 to reveal the answer to our first mystery. Tajiri Satoshi, *Pokémon*'s creator, had a very fruitful first encounter with the Game Boy. While people were immediately drawn to the screen of the portable device Tajiri was inspired by a humbler element of the console; its Link Cable. He imagined little insects travelling along the wire, going from one Game Boy to the other. From this simple idea *Pokémon* was born. At least that's the myth, told time and time again by Satoshi to explain the genesis of his concept.

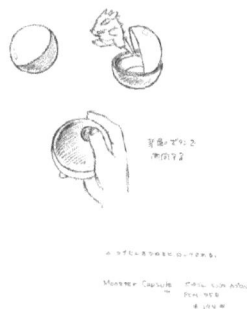

I'm a bit skeptical of this perfect story absent of any influence from other video games. He knew video games well and I refuse to believe Satoshi wasn't influenced by *Makai Toushi SaGa*. Known in the West as *The Final Fantasy Legend*, it's the first role-playing game for the system coming in a mere six months after the system's initial release. It showed that the Game Boy was a perfect system for RPGs. I covered it previously, and I marvelled at how it attempted so much, so early in the system's life. The game features monsters in your party, that can evolve (and devolve) based on eating the meat of your defeated enemies. I'm inclined to believe that Satoshi played *Makai Toushi SaGa* and got some inspiration from the game. Perhaps he even dreamed not of insects travelling along the wire but of the monsters in *Makai Toushi SaGa*.

I don't want to diminish the accomplishments, especially since the monster trading is a novel idea worth all the praise it has gotten, but there is this tendency with developers, and Japanese developers in particular to shy away from mentioning inspirations from other video games. All we can do is presume which is what I'm doing here.

What Did Game Freak Publish Before Making Video Games?

Satoshi was a publisher of a fanzine focusing on arcade titles which he worked on alongside Sugimori Ken, the artist drawing the fanzine's art. Ken would later become the main artist for the game.

I saw some original copies of their fanzine in a museum exhibit and they were underwhelming. There's no magical quality to them; they were low quality Japanese fanzines made with a lot of love but still simply fanzines. Those little staples books are relevant because they birthed Game Freak and put Satoshi and Ken together allowing them to later pivot to video game development.

Which Surprising Pokémon Was Born First?

The original concept for Capsule Monsters, which would become *Pocket Monsters* before release, used generic creatures that looked like dragons and dinosaurs. Amongst those dinosaur-looking creatures, one has been identified as the first Pokémon, the first creature that was imagined during this early concept and survived all the way to the release of the game.

Rhydon was the oldest design to end up in the final game. He is a very generic-looking dinosaur with a rhinoceros horn, so it makes a ton of sense that he is the oldest Pokémon, coming from the era where all the creatures were inspired by dinosaurs. More creative concepts like Electabuzz would come later.

△ 洞窟探険

Hey look who's in the back of this very early sketch.

What Horrible NES Game Funded the Development of Pokémon?

Once again I have to make a personal connection before I answer the question because I'm a raging narcissist. When the Super Nintendo came out, I didn't have one. I had gotten a second-hand NES earlier in the year so of course my mother was not about to start upgrading her six-year-old son with the latest and greatest. Since I was smitten with Yoshi and dreamed of nothing but riding him in *Super Mario World*, I asked my mom to buy me *Yoshi* for NES as a birthday gift. When I started playing it this is what I saw.

It's a shitty puzzle game. To rub even more salt in the

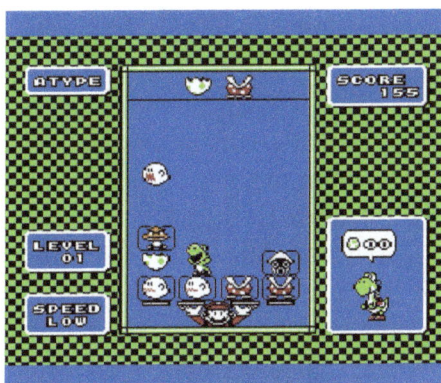

What a giant piece of shit.

wound, there's a better Yoshi puzzle game, *Yoshi's Cookie*, and *Yoshi* is not even half as good as *Yoshi's Cookie*. It's just terribly uninspired and boring.

So what's the Pokémon connection? Game Freak was cash poor during the early '90s, and Nintendo bailed them out because they believed in their Pocket Monsters concept. I think part of the help they got from Nintendo was to be assigned to develop *Yoshi*. This allowed them to make enough money on a surefire hit based on a hot new character, and to learn the complicated details of video game development. They could keep going and maintain the development of *Pokémon* using the money they made from *Yoshi*.

Now I can sleep at night knowing that I directly financed the development of Pokémon all the way back in 1992. Well, I guess my mom financed the development of *Pokémon*. Be sure to thank my mom if you see her.

Who Really Owns the Pokémon Franchise?

When *Pokémon Go* was initially released on iOS and became **the** global phenomenon of the summer of 2016, Nintendo's stock in the Tokyo stock Exchange suddenly doubled. Nintendo, unfortunately, could not enjoy this sudden excitement for their stock. Because they knew that investors would cool when they learned that Nintendo is not the master of the Pokémon franchise. They clarified their complicated relationship with Pokémon Go, and the stock went back down. It's obvious they were scared the stock would fall **harder** once the game was monetized and Nintendo would make no money from the game. You see, Nintendo didn't make *Pokémon Go*, and they don't even wholly own the Pokémon franchise. In fact, they do not receive direct revenue from *Pokémon*. What? Nintendo doesn't outright own Pokémon? Then who does? Three companies do, with a fourth special case, and let's go through each one.

Game Freak

The OG gang, the company created by Tajiri Satoshi, Masuda Jun'ichi, and Sugimori Ken to publish their fanzine that later transitioned to video game development. It is at this company that Tajiri created the whole Pokémon concept and it is still to this day the birthplace of any new concept or monster. No other developer or licensee can willy-nilly create a new Pokémon called Pikatwo; Game Freak is the sole place where new Pokémon are birthed. They have stayed a small developer, even though they're the idea factory of the largest media franchise in the world. The small size is seemingly to foster creativity and maintain a high level of control. Whenever anybody complains that the graphics in a Pokémon game are terrible, their minuscule size is the reason. They simply do not have the manpower to rival the bigger studios inside Nintendo.

Like I just mentioned, they're the company responsible for the development of Pokémon games but only what is usually called the core games; think *Pokémon Sun* or *Pokémon Legends: Arceus*. Altough that distinction is getting muddled, with the latest remakes, *Brilliant Diamond* and *Shining Pearl* being developed by ILCA, a relatively obscure Japanese developer. Quick aside, they obviously delegated those two remakes to ILCA to work as much as possible on *Pokémon Legends: Arceus*, a top to bottom reinvention of the game concept. With once again terrible graphics.

Nintendo

Between the birth of the idea from the mind of Tajiri Satoshi and the release of the first game in 1996, Game Freak presented the project to Nintendo and the company became its publisher. Nintendo also acquired a stake in the franchise itself. This is particular since a publisher does not necessarily own the intellectual property of the game it publishes: you can look at *Banjo-Kazooie* for example, initially published by Nintendo in the '90s but now available on Microsoft consoles. This could happen because the company that made the game, Rare, did not sell the ownership of the copyright to Nintendo even though Nintendo owned a controlling stake in Rare; they instead collaborated on the development and distribution. If I had to hazard a guess as to why Nintendo bought a stake in the Pokémon franchise itself I'd say it's because Game Freak needed the money to finish the game.

In direct terms, Nintendo shares the Pokémon copyright with the other three companies holding it. It shares the trademark in Japan with those three companies and is the sole owner of the trademark in the rest of the world. Don't forget to look up the difference between a copyright and a trademark kids. This share of the franchise means Nintendo considers *Pokémon* its own: Pikachu and the rest were in *Super*

Smash Bros. from the first game's release.

To most people everything related to Pokémon is made by Nintendo when the truth is far more complicated. Nintendo's not even the sole publisher of the Pokémon games on Nintendo's own consoles. They share that role with the Pokémon Company that they also happen to co-own with the other companies with which it shares the Pokémon copyright. I told you it was complicated.

Creatures Inc.

Who is Creatures Inc. exactly? It makes sense that Game Freak and Nintendo share the franchise, but why is there a third company in the mix? According to Masuda Junichi, a co-founder of Game Freak and the current creative overseer for the games, they were the producers of the first game. This is strange since the producer of a game is usually a person working for the company making the game, not an outside company. Thinking about the situation, I don't think they'll ever admit it, but I think Creatures Inc. was brought in to help Tajiri finish the game. He couldn't do it alone since he had never produced a game before: he was a fanzine writer.

The history of Creatures Inc. also seems to confirm my thinking. Creatures Inc. is made-up of former employees of Ape Inc. who supported a visionary artist with no video game experience to produce a very personal RPG based on a fairy-tale version of our modern world. I'm of course not talking of *Pokémon* but of Itoi Shigesato and his game *Mother*, which we know in the West as *Earthbound Beginnings*. It turns out the employees of Creatures Inc. helped with the same job twice!

Since they helped finish the first Pokémon game their contract clearly gave them partial ownership of the franchise, and they went on to create the Pokémon trading card game (it wasn't made by Wizards of the Coast who simply localized it) and other elements of the franchise. Once again if I had to guess as to why Creatures own a part of the franchise it's because Game Freak couldn't pay them to help them, so they paid them with a franchise stake.

The Pokémon Company

Created by all three above companies to initially manage the *Pokémon Center* stores popping up in Japan in the early '90s, it quickly became the company managing the licensing of Pokémon. So if a toiletry company wants to put Pikachu on a towel, they call The Pokémon Company, not Nintendo. The question arises, though: why not let Nintendo manage the licensing?

These days, Nintendo is good at licensing its characters for interesting products. I'm particularly impressed by the Mario Lego sets, with its special Mario Lego character with screens for eyes, a small speaker and an NFC reader allowing him to emote and react to specially tagged bricks. Or *Mario Kart Live*, the toy that allows you to kart race in your own home. In the mid '90s, however, Nintendo was only able to give adequate focus to the Japanese market. Licensed Nintendo products overseas like toys, cereals, books, or content like TV shows and movies were all terrible. In a recent reunion organized by the VGHF, Gail Tilden, first editor-in-chief of Nintendo Power Magazine mentioned that licensing at Nintendo throughout the '90s was barebones and that the magazine had to producing its own marketing material.

So I don't believe Nintendo was prepared to deal with Pokémon: they never managed to license anything worthwhile related to *The Legend of Zelda*, for example. They were a toy maker, not a licensing manager. So a fourth company was emboldened to manage everything related to licensed Pokémon products.

The Pokémon Company now even co-publishes the games

on Nintendo consoles and has become the sort of brand manager for Pokémon in its entirety, managing tournaments, products, and announcements related to the franchise. So they have never stopped growing their importance as time went on. If one company is responsible for the successes and mistakes made with the franchise now, it's them.

Why Does the Game Have a Green Version in Japan?

Upon its initial release in Japan the two versions of the game were the red and green versions. Most people are aware of this regional difference in versions since the remakes on Game Boy Advance feature those original colours but I still feel compelled to explain it.

One fascinating invention of Pokémon is the concept of the dual versions. To foster the trading of monsters between players, the game came in two flavours, green and red, with a specific subset of Pokémon unique to each game. This meant that to complete your Pokédex (that you owned one copy of every creature) you have to trade with someone else. Someone with a different version. There isn't an overwhelming list of Pokémon unique to each version, just a handful, but it taught everyone that Pokémon is about trading with other players.

As the Japanese in early 1996 were going crazy over those two initial versions, *Pocket Monsters: Red* and *Pocket Monsters: Green*, players also discovered the game had some rough edges. The graphics were clunky, the monsters didn't look exactly the same as in the manual illustrations, and the game had some unfortunate bugs. A version that featured updated graphics and fixed some of the bugs was released later in 1996. This was called *Pocket Monsters: Blue*. All the later localization work was based on this improved game so no one outside Japan ever saw the original graphics. They kept the original monster distribution from Japanese Red for international Red, and transposed the Green distribution into the international Blue version. At this point, why not go all the way and localize Green instead? I guess Blastoise has cannons, that's too cool to pass up.

We'll talk about Yellow in its own article.

Why Did It Take Two Years for the Game to Be Localized and Released in North America?

This one is easy to answer: *Dragon Quest*. Back in the days of the Famicom, *Dragon Quest* seduced the Japanese with its quirky reinvention of the role-playing game. By *Dragon Quest III*, the series was a societal phenomenon. Enix famously moved releases to Saturdays, to alleviate public concerns from some Diet legislators.

Pocket Monsters was obviously going in the same direction in Japan. Everybody and their mother knew about the game and anything related to the franchise was a guaranteed smash hit. But there was one major flaw with *Dragon Quest*: no one cared about it outside of Japan. It had its fans but Nintendo was directly stung by its poor North American reception. They published the localization in North America and had such a sale dud that they had to give the cartridges with Nintendo Power subscriptions to get rid of their unsold copies.

This failure led to years of statements by employees of Nintendo that non-Japanese players didn't like RPGs. They weren't wrong; RPGs sold far less in North America than in Japan, but it was a chicken or the egg situation. RPGs had a ton of text to localize, which meant a protracted localization process, and used far more memory, which all meant a more expensive product. For these reasons few Japanese RPGs were localized and brought West meaning it was much harder to build an audience for the few games that did see a release. When Nintendo tried their hands at bringing RPGs to North America they always had disappointing results. *Earthbound* left a particularly sour taste to everyone involved at Nintendo of America according to *Pokémon* translator Nob Ogasawara. It was very difficult to translate with *Mother* creator Itoi Shigesato getting directly involved and sold very poorly, killing any hope to reverse the trend of underperforming RPGs with *Earthbound*.

This illustrates how careful everyone at Nintendo was regarding *Pocket Monsters*. It was yet another reinvention of the role-playing game and the same lack of interest for the genre could hurt them once again, just like *Dragon Quest* and *Mother/Earthbound*.

They had to try releasing it outside Japan, it would be ridiculous not to, but they wanted to take their time to get it right. They considered redesigning the creatures to increase their *western* appeal but ultimately abandoned the idea. Time was ticking and on top of that the industry had started to change since the release of *Dragon Warrior*. We were now under the auspices of an entertainment model. In effect, the marketing challenge for game publishers had shifted. Before, you had to get a consumer to buy your game. Now, you had to get a retailer to stock your game in the first place.

> Starting around 1994, the software industry transitioned to what Nina Schulyer called the *entertainment model* of marketing. If retail shelf space was harder to come by and lasted for a shorter time, the idea was to put more resources into generating hype in advance, raising awareness for the title before it was even released, the same way Hol-

lywood studios promoted movies. [...] It's no co-incidence that right around this time also marked the beginning of Electronic Entertainment Expo (E3), a massive game industry marketing event that was originally intended as a way to advertise directly to retailers.

Excerpt of *The incredible boxes of Hock Wah Yeo* from The Obscuritory.

Nintendo could not put a game on the shelves and spend months hyping it like they did in 1989 with *Dragon Warrior*; retailers did not have the patience for that. Considering the original *Pocket Monsters* in Japan became a phenomenon through word of mouth and needed months to reach its sale potential, it benefitted greatly from the old model where the game sat on shelves waiting for consumers.

So Nintendo, Game Freak and Creatures wisely prepared something special for the release of Pokémon. Nintendo internally translated most of the core concepts of the game and would then use those translated Pokémon names and concepts for the anime localization. Those two products, game and anime, would both release together in the fall of 1998. A one-two punch of Pokémon content, which would hopefully entice american children. For good measure, the surprisingly successful Trading Card Game would follow the next spring, distributed by Wizards of the Coast, the people behind *Magic: The Gathering*.

It took them a while to arrive at this plan, and required a lot of effort to implement. History vindicated their patience.

How Did Pokémon Teach Me About the Idiosyncratic Québec Media Landscape?

I was 10 in 1996 when *Pocket Monsters* was released in Japan. I was still playing with my Game Boy even though it felt like the rest of the world had moved on. Games were still available but the recent releases left me unimpressed. I focused my attention on playing older releases whenever I could.

But I started hearing a rumour, from magazines and video game TV shows, about this new Game Boy title made by Nintendo (no one ever mentioned Game Freak back then). A game were you explored a world full of monsters. You captured and befriended those monsters to fight other trainers, never fighting them yourself.

I obviously knew that Nintendo and all my favourite video games were made in Japan but here was rare news about an exciting **Game Boy** title. The really crazy part, though, was that the game was a massive cultural phenomenon in Japan. The news and articles were saying that everyone was playing it. What? Everybody was playing a Game Boy game in 1996? It was unbelievable to my young brain. I thought I was the only person still playing the Game Boy.

You have to do a bit of mental work here, dear reader, to forget the existence of Pokémon. It's not an easy thing to do. Pokémon is according to most metrics the most profitable media franchise **ever**.

You think the Marvel Cinematic Universe is bigger? Nope. They don't have much reach outside the movies and TV shows themselves so it's not enough revenue to compete.

Star Wars, with its forty years of associated toy sales? It's not enough of a success outside North America, particularly in Asia, to compete. Star Wars is perhaps bigger than Poké-mon in the US, but not worldwide.

Star Trek? The Pokémon trading card game alone is bigger than all of Star Trek at an estimated ten billion dollars in card revenue since its release.

Pokémon is simply the biggest media franchise ever, and it's as relevant now all around the globe in 2022 as it has ever been. But there was a time before Pokémon was a global phenomenon. For a time, it was strictly a Japanese affair. The rest of the world could only stay outside, trying to look inside. And we're not talking months here. Pokémon remained a Japanese phenomenon for two years. The rest of the world could only get an outside glimpse at the craze for a very long time. The trading card game, a Nintendo 64 game that allowed you to fight using the Pokémon from your Game Boy cartridge, a manga, the anime, even the first movie were all released before the Poké-phenomenom left Japan.

Pokémon was finally released in North America in the Fall of 1998, and it promptly flew over my head. I didn't notice it was released. I was unaware that the Japanese phenomenon had finally crossed the Pacific. I didn't even know they had decided on *Pokémon* as its English name. How could that be? *Pokémon* was released in North America along with the anime. It was everywhere. How could I completely miss this release? Before I answer that question, let's move forward in time to early 1999, when I saw the best video game publicity ever made.

Super Smash Bros. came out in April of 1999 and I bought it as soon as possible with my hard-earned paperboy money. *Super Smash Bros.* obviously features Pikachu, and even Jigglypuff, as playable characters. There's a stage from the franchise as well, and you can even use Pokéballs. I immediately got very curious once I started playing. There's a yellow electric rat constantly screaming his own name that's given

Strictly based on this ad's sense of humour, I decided to buy the game.

as much reverence as gaming Jesus, our lord and stomper, Mario. What was the deal with that? So I remembered all those rumblings about the pocket monster game, and figured that the game must be this Pokémon thing I was seeing in *Smash*. When I looked at the Works section in Pikachu's character sheet, his single released game was there.

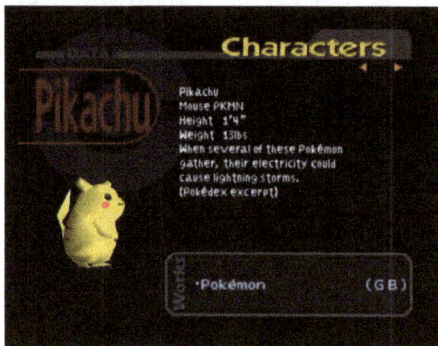

That's how old I am kids. I learned that Pokémon was released from the *Super Smash Bros.* character biographies.

I finally ended up seeing both the *Red* and *Blue* games at my local Zellers. How could I miss the media onslaught of

Pokémon and being surprised at the presence of Pikachu in *Super Smash Bros.*?

Because I'm Québécois. In Québec, the language barrier meant we got some stuff later than the United States and Canada. Big popular movies came out dubbed in French at basically the same time but books and especially TV shows were on a different timeframe as the rest of North America. An American TV show had to become popular enough to warrant shopping it around internationally, then it has to be licensed and dubbed by a Québec TV network and only then can it be put on their schedule.

Don't go thinking that Québec always uses dubs made in France. A lot of French dubs for movies and TV shows are meant to be used internationally; they'll use language understandable across *la francophonie*, and use a toned down Parisian accent informally called international French. These dubs are common in Québec for movies and TV shows but not all dubbing follows these constraints. Comedic and lighthearted content, like a Japanese anime about a boy capturing local wildlife in red balls, is better served by a local dub since it can more accurately reflect the local inflection and sense of humour.

Doing a cursory investigation tells me that Québec would usually get popular American TV shows a year later than in the US during the '80s and '90s, whether a French or Québec dub was used. That is if the show came to Québec at all. Some TV shows were never broadcast in Québec, and others, like American single-camera sitcoms were never popular in Québec. They're cheap to make, so Québec produced its own sitcoms that were more popular than the American ones. Shows like *Friends* or *Seinfeld* were not particularly popular here in large part due to their use of a French from France dub.

But the overwhelming majority of video games were not

translated at the time (publishers were finally required by law to offer French versions of their games in 2007) and would come out at the same time in both markets. This led to interesting situations in Québec. For example, the Capcom game of *Chip 'n Dale: Rescue Rangers* for NES was available **before** the cartoon was broadcast on TV. This was absolutely normal for me and all my friends back then.

As a final aside, the situation has changed considerably in recent times; I vividly remember being astonished in 2006 that the show *Lost* was broadcast in French on Radio-Canada only six weeks after the original version had aired on ABC in the US. Nowadays, the lead time for dubbed versions has been reduced even further. The greatest example is *Game of Thrones*, which was available in 170 countries on the same day during its last few seasons. On the other hand, most broadcast (ie. non-streaming) media still has some lead time before the release of its dub in Québec and other international markets. Depending on the property the French dub might be used, without a proper local Québec dub.

So why am I telling you all this? Because the *Pokémon* anime arrived in Québec in the fall of 1999, one year after the game's release in 1998. I missed the media onslaught because there was no media onslaught. North America was not like Europe where companies would coordinate multiple localization when releasing there. North America back then meant a strictly English release, with local Québec broadcasters left to fend for themselves. In the case of Pokémon, the translators waited a year to use the scripts from France, but dubbed the anime with Québec voice artists, using the English Pokémon name but the localized town and location names used in France. I think this is in large part because the game was only available in English in Québec; we were already familiar with names like Jynx, so French names like Lippoutou were deemed innapropriate.

This made Québec the only region in the world to use the English Pokémon name in another language. Nowadays Québec has lost its local dub; the dub from France is unfortunately used. This means that Québec is also the only region in the world where the names of the creatures suddenly changed! With the now common practice of releasing games across North America in English, Spanish, and French, Lippoutou is now *de rigueur*.

Are There More Than 150 Pokémon?

Of course there have been more than 150 Pokémon for a long time, but were there more than the 150 Pokémon upon the initial release? And maybe more importantly, why does it even matter? It matters because there was indeed a hidden Pokémon only accessible through special events or outright cheating. This created an aura of mystery around the game. Since the original Pokémon is also riddled with bugs, causing all sorts of glitches to occur, players started seeing all sort of weird things they falsely prescribed to intended secret monsters.

That real hidden Pokémon was Mew, designed and hidden by Morimoto Shigeki the programmer of the game, as a kind of prank that only he could access and share with his colleagues. Mew was, of course, mentioned in the game (Mew**two** was in the game after all) but the creature was not meant to be seen. Once the rest of the team learned of the existence of Mew they started officially distributing the creature during events. This meant it was rare for Japanese players to receive a Mew and bred the interest in finding ways, fake or not, to catch Mew. Look up the legends surrounding the truck in Vermillion City. I remember having to hear all about that truck and feeling so bad for the people who wholeheartedly believed Mew was hidden under there.

Mixing into this desire for the real hidden monster, the game was riddled with bugs and bogus glitches allowed one to capture creatures that were the result of memory corruption. The most famous of these was *MissingNo.* and I remember schoolmates showing me the glitch all the way back in 1999. That sure didn't help people differantiate truth from fiction; if you could catch a glitched Pokémon by surfing alongside a border of the map, why couldn't you catch a Mew under a truck?

A year after the game's release, idle theories and useful glitches, like the candy duplication trick, were already widely shared amongst players even in the depths of Lac-Saint-Jean.

Is the Game Any Good?

You've always had to bring your own fun into a *Pokémon* title. No hand-holding can change the fact that the core games have always been about deciding on your own what's fun for you. Do you want to create an unbeatable team? What about playing through the story with a team of six Jigglypuff? Maybe you're interested in collecting every monster? Perhaps your interest lies in the thrill of competing against your friends? Or maybe trading with your friends? *Pokémon* really shines when you can define an objective for yourself. I have only experienced *Pokémon* as a solo endeavour, with the goal of completing the game, since no one cared about it when I picked it up to help me spice things up. So it was kind of boring for me. Once the *Pokémon* anime hit the Québec airwaves, and a group of kids at school started playing the game during lunch, I had moved on.

If you pick it up in 2022, you'll have a tough task ahead of you; you'll have to figure out how to have fun with that game. It's a difficult endeavour getting harder: I mean, *Pokémon Legends: Arceus* is right there, ready to entertain you effortlessly, albeit with terrible graphics.

Pokémon Legends: Arceus notwithstanding, every new adventure had been an improvement over the previous game, never a reinvention. So going back in time and playing the earlier titles is difficult. Perhaps if a feature you loved was removed there was reason to walk back the route. But nostalgia is the powerful drug that keeps people coming back to the first title. When they do, those people have to contend with so many irritants. For one, the game is excruciatingly slow. Everything takes forever. You walk slow, the menus are slow, the animations are slow, the text scrolls slowly, saving is slow. Nothing is fast, and the game feels fragile as a result. It feels like you can't push the buttons on your Game Boy too hard or the game will break under the load. Considering the game is infamous for its buggy code it's warranted. After all, they famously abandoned their old code base and rewrote everything when they released *Pokémon Ruby & Sapphire* on Game Boy Advance.

If you can get past the disrespect that game has for your time, which is a tough pill to swallow, you'll find a quirky fun RPG with a wicked concept: no creature in the game is only an enemy. You can ultimately train and befriend your own Muk, or Lapras, or Zapdos. You can then use those monsters to trade and battle with your friends, using the connectivity afforded by the link cable. When it released, multiplayer experiences were far more niche than they are today. Online multiplayer, with services like Battle.net, were embryonic and riddled with issues and massively multiplayer online games were the purview of the committed few. The multiplayer concept was unique. No other game allowed you to trade creatures with your friends. Heck, even nowadays the concept is unique with nary a serious competitor to Game Freak in sight.

Conclusion

Only on Game Boy could Pokémon become such a large hit. The confluence of a large installed base with the ubiquity of the link cable made the gigantic hit a possibility. No other video game platform was as perfectly positioned to deliver the biggest media franchise in the world. That is what makes discussing everything around *Pokémon* interesting for me. I don't believe for one second that *Pokémon* could have happened on Super Famicom or any other console. The core idea of trading monsters with friends would have needed a technological solution that Game Freak was incapable of developing since they were such a small studio. After seven years of Game Boy, *Pokémon* finally fulfilled the possibilities of the link cable. It was suddenly cool that portable consoles offered device-to-device multiplayer. Even today, the Switch is capable of playing a local game and trading monsters with another Switch next to it without any internet access needed. You can't do that with two PlayStations or two Xboxes.

Another important aspect was the incredibly long legs of the concept. You couldn't shake the idea that sequels were inevitable while playing the first game. Exploring Kanto, you could imagine other regions with other completely different monsters just outside the realm of your Game Boy screen. It's not a surprise that an anime, a trading card game and other video games were easily developed once Pokémon hit it big: its concept is versatile and can be adapted to almost anything. Case in point, they made a Pokémon detective movie.

Finally, Pokémon made the Game Boy cool again, to everybody's surprise. Game Boy hardware sales massively picked up once *Pokémon* was released. That meant that there was a renewed interest in the console. Around the world, old Game Boy development kits were cleaned of their cobwebs, and a massive amount of new titles started development. With the hindsight of years of experience with the platform, and the inspiration from *Pokémon* to innovate, the overall quality of those new games was surprising. The Game Boy went from also-ran to exciting within a year.

It also happened to be the only console where you could make a *Pokémon* ripoff, since no other popular system could allow trades between cartridges. All of that gave the Game Boy a renaissance that no console ever had, or ever will. The Game Boy was reborn thanks to those little insects walking up and down the link cable.

Mole Mania

- Japanese release in July 1996
- North American release in February 1997
- European release in 1997
- Published by Nintendo
- Developed by Nintendo EAD & Pax Softnica

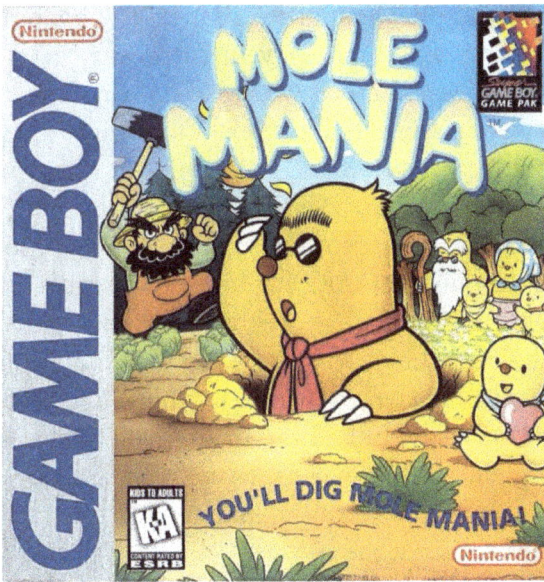

It's a mole with glasses!

Buried Treasure

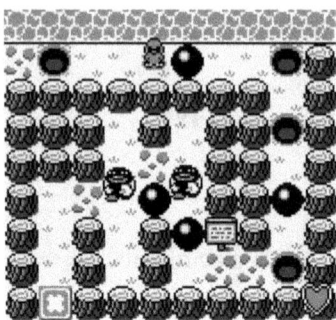

Yokoi Gunpei, the father of the Game Boy, was in a weird spot. He was the company's oldest team leader at Nintendo but his reputation was shot. Inside the company he was seen as having lost his way, having spent too much of the company's time and effort on a failed project with no appeal, the dreadful Virtual Boy. It was the epitome of his creed of using old technology in surprising ways (usually translated as *Lateral Thinking with Withered Technology*) but it lacked the fun factor that made Nintendo into a household name resulting in a very public failure for the company. Yokoi had planned on leaving Nintendo right after the release of the Virtual Boy. His interest in seeing the new console to release was the only thing keeping him at Nintendo. With that project a burning red failure, Yokoi stayed; he wanted to leave on a positive note, not in disgrace. To that end, he looked at the original Game Boy. It ran laps around the competition of portable consoles but all the media outlets were wondering why there was no new hardware. The answer was pure Nintendo: they were intent on maintaining the same principle that made the Game Boy a success of not compromising on battery life. Since there was no new CPU or screen tech that would provide a better experience while maintaining a reasonable battery life, Yokoi Gunpei tasked himself and his team with making a better version of the already existing Game Boy. This project would ultimately lead to the Game Boy Pocket.

While Nintendo kept the same muted, simple strategy for its portable behemoth, Game Boy games were getting rarer. To keep shelves stocked with good games Nintendo started their Players' Choice program. *The Legend of Zelda: Link's Awakening, Star Wars, The Bugs Bunny Crazy Castle, Mega Man: Dr. Wily's Revenge* are just some examples of games republished by Nintendo under their Players' Choice banner. Clearly, the company was trying to put older titles of better quality on store shelves to maintain interest for the Game Boy and its new upgrade the Game Boy Pocket.

While in Japan *Pokémon* was out since February of '96, the global future was uncertain. It was a truly gangbuster success locally that had given a second wind to the Game Boy but could this success be replicated outside Japan? Could Game Freak, an unproven group of young inexperienced people, provide more Pokémon games to solidify the mania? How long would people buy Game Boy systems to play *Pokémon*? Nothing was certain. Out of this weird middle age for the Game Boy, Game Boy Pocket was born. With that new console revision came one marquee title to coincide with the release, the fourth and final Nintendo EAD developed game for Game Boy: *Mole Mania*. A puzzle game pitting you as a mole that pushes and throws things while digging holes, the best way to describe it would be to compare it to the action puzzle games of the '80s like *Sokoban* or *Lode Runner*.

I cannot say it loud enough: play this game! *Mole Mania* is very good. It's a Miyamoto Shigeru masterpiece done during his golden age when his output was arguably at his summit. He was supervising classics like *Yoshi's Island* and *Super Mario 64* and here comes this game done in a genre that he had abandoned, and he brings all the lessons he learned since he last made an action puzzle game. It's a true bona fide classic, and it's absolutely **forgotten**.

A Hole Game

Since this is a top-of-the-line Miyamoto game all the bad things about action puzzle games are smoothed out. There are so many pitfalls the game could have fallen into but you can see they play-tested the hell out of the game to make it fun. Unlike *Lode Runner*, the enemies of the game stick to predictable patterns. They never run toward you, Terminator-style, making you run for your life every instant. Instead, **you** get in **their** way, because they follow a pattern.

There's always a short way to reset a puzzle. Like *Sokoban* you can get objects stuck but there's a very simple way to reset a puzzle. You just leave the screen and come back. A menu option also exists.

Every puzzle has the same solution: push the black ball against the rock blocking the path to the next screen. So you can fixate on getting that ball where it needs to go. There are multiple objects you can push but they always gravitate around getting out of the black ball's way. However, the game often gives you more objects than you need. A pipe elbow will be pointless and irrelevant to the solution of the puzzle. Thus, puzzles are not always *clean*, meaning that you have more than what you need to finish it. On top of that, there are sometimes multiple methods to clear an exit. This is particularly apparent in level 4, where you have in quick succession multiple types of puzzles. So when reaching a new screen you immediately need to figure out whether there are objects that are useless to complete the level.

The game's core gameplay is a throwback to games like *Devil's World* and other early Famicom titles. Like those games it's a single-screen affair, very interested in providing time-sensitive puzzles and filled with unbeatable enemies that need to be avoided. It's a game that reflects back on the era when everybody was improving on the *Pac-Man* formula. *Mole Mania* should have happened in the '80s when you look at its lineage and genre but everything else about the game is very 1996. The presentation is flawless, the game is littered with valuable secrets. It has boss battles and bonus stages and the ability to be played somewhat non-sequentially so you can come back later to a puzzle that stumps you. All elements that were common by 1996.

It feels like Miyamoto was thinking of an interesting project to do and saying *I know how to do this effortlessly* and **he actually does**. The presentation is as good as any mid 90s era SNES or N64 game with its distinct worlds, story told through the environment, and anime-inspired premise. *Mole Mania* is what happens when a developer goes back to older concepts and looks at those old tropes with their improved experience. Miyamoto knew how to push the contractors at Pax Softnica, with which he had already released two other Game Boy games, to refine the concepts until they were flawless, he knew how to remove anything superfluous so the game was easy to understand, and he knew how to build on his simple idea until it became delightfully hard while keeping its original core concept. Miyamoto in 1984, when he originally made games that look like *Mole Mania* was not **that** good. It might be my bias but I think *Mole Mania* is Miyamoto at his best. It was made in the same era as *Super Mario 64*, Nintendo EAD's masterpiece. I can imagine a stressed out Miyamoto coming out of a difficult *Super Mario 64* design meeting and going to speak to the people making *Mole Mania* afterwards to relax with something relatively simple. Something where he already knew how to solve the problems, where he wasn't confronted with 3D problems he had no idea existed and still had to figure out. Imagine how much easier it is to work on *Mole Mania* when you spent the whole day trying to figure out how to control the camera in *Super Mario 64*.

Conclusion

The original Game Boy is at its best with this game; to me *Mole Mania* is a gift. I've adored Miyamoto's trifecta of the late '90s: *Yoshi's Island*, which he believed to be his last 2D platformer, *Super Mario 64*, his success at inventing how to jump and explore a 3D world, and *The Legend of Zelda: Ocarina of Time*, the refinement of everything learned making those two other games. I thought I had played all his games made during that era, but here we have a fourth albeit lesser work done with the same talent by the same man and I had never played it. I can't bring myself to finish *Mole Mania*; when I'm done I won't have any games from golden age Miyamoto.

As a last aside, *Mole Mania* gives a great example against the concept of console generations to classify video games. Go read about video game history on Wikipedia for example or pick up any lesser book and you'll be very quickly presented with this idea of console generations defining the whole industry. It's everywhere, to the point where developers themselves constantly discuss their work in the context of generations. While generations can make some sense if only TV consoles existed, portable systems exist and are just as important. A game like *Mole Mania* and any Game Boy game released in 1996 is considered in the same goddamn generation as the Famicom released in 1983. *Mole Mania* was developed by Miyamoto concurrently with *Super Mario 64*. Both titles are brethrens, directed by the same man at the same time. No one should consider those games two generations apart. So that's why I'm against the concept of generations, which is player-centric, while video games are made by artists. Artistic considerations and mindsets are more important than marketing categorization. *Mole Mania* embodies that idea perfectly.

Kirby's Dream Land

- Japanese release in April 1992
- North American release in August 1992
- European release in 1992
- Published by Nintendo
- Developed by HAL Laboratory

Pink is in.

A Little Piece of Perfection

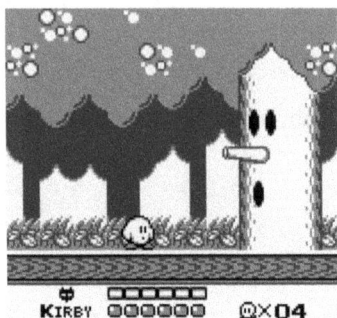

Close your eyes for just a moment. Imagine a quiet green plain with a comforting wind slowly swaying the grass back and forth. Near the horizon there are rose-coloured mountains. Just go along with it, rose mountains are normal. Taking in the heat of the sun's rays (the sun has a face, once again it's totally normal), in the swaying grass is the most serene and sweet character our imagination can muster. It's asleep, lightly snoring as its basking in the warm glow of the beautiful day. Just like the mountains it's pink. It's Kirby. A pink ball of niceness with shoes and cute stubby arms. Its only default is its voraciousness, but it manages to make that cute too.

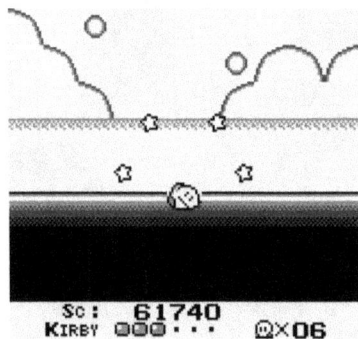

Nowadays, the character's cheery attitude has been turned into a bit of an ironic in-joke. He's the cutest, with him being pink and always happy, but he's also the most badass! The ultimate evil of the universe managed to destroy every single character in the introduction of *Super Smash Bros. Ultimate* but Kirby survived all that. *Because, you see, it's a secret badass.* However, the character was initially created without irony; the gumdrop aesthetic was honest. Kirby was not secretly all-powerful even though it looked harmless. There was no subversion of our expectations. In fact, the aesthetic was a core marketing element of Kirby's first game. This evolution of Kirby's character can perhaps be explained by the disconnect between the world of Kirby and the actions it performs. All the verbs at your disposal in *Kirby's Dream Land* are indistinguishable from a mature, violent side-scroller platformer like *Contra* if only Bill and Lance could fly.

SOAR.

DEVOUR.

EMPOWER.

SHOOT.

ATTACK.

DEFEAT.

You relentlessly move forward mercilessly destroying your enemies by swallowing them and throwing their remains at other enemies. The visuals make it a fun jaunt and everyone is happy and cute. Isn't that wonderful, and essential?

Setting the Stage

Kirby is the quintessential Nintendo character but it is not a Nintendo creation. It is not even owned by Nintendo; HAL Laboratory owns the rights. How can Kirby be a quintessential Nintendo icon if it's owned by another company?

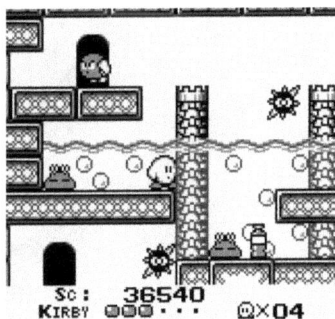

HAL Laboratory always had a close relationship with Nintendo going all the way back to the Famicom. When the console was initially conceived,

Nintendo had few programmers to make games for its first console with interchangeable software. The savvy people working at Nintendo turned to the people of small company HAL who were able to help out, particularly due to one of their younger programmers, Iwata Satoru. He, along with his other colleagues, were commissioned by Nintendo to work on seminal Famicom titles like *Golf, Balloon Fight*, and *Pinball*. Their contributions stayed hidden; neither their company nor their names appeared on those Nintendo titles. When the '90s rolled around, however, HAL had gotten in an impossible position. Their prestige 1991 Famicom game *Metal Slader Glory* was unprofitable and they were caught in a financial death spiral. Nintendo's executives saw potential in HAL and bailed the company (presumably for a controlling stake) but asked that Iwata Satoru, who by this point had gotten a great reputation as a manager, become the new company president. All in all, a quintessential Yamauchi Hiroshi move. This would turn out to be the most important personnel move Yamauchi ever did; Iwata got so respected he ended up succeeding Yamauchi at the helm of the whole of Nintendo a decade later.

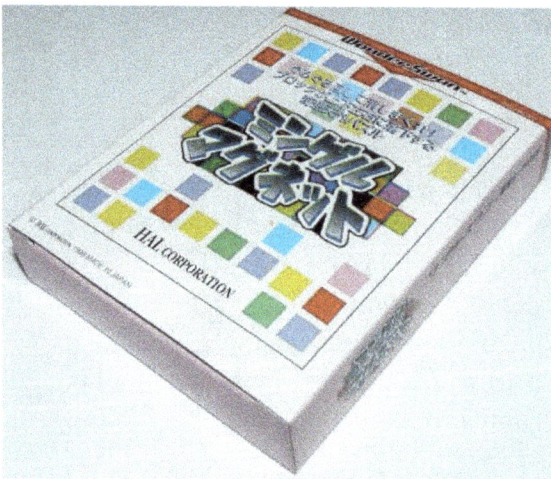

Mingle Magnet for Wonderswan

Nintendo has tightened its control over HAL Laboratory ever since that fateful 1991 death spiral with the last work of HAL not published on a Nintendo console, *Mingle Magnet* for Wonderswan, released in 1999. They now seem to be a fully owned subsidiary which makes them what is commonly termed a second-party developer. However, back when they made *Kirby's Dream Land* they were in the process of being bailed by Nintendo. Sakurai Masahiro talked about his experience of working for a company going through bankruptcy in his *Kirby's Adventure* development video on his YouTube channel. Kirby is the child of this marriage of convenience.

Creating a Placeholder

The father of Kirby, Sakurai Masahiro, was 19 when he created Kirby. He had only one other game credit under his belt, also with HAL; the interesting but obscure Game Boy shooter *Trax*. Since Nintendo now had a hand in the management of HAL, Yamauchi Hiroshi, the ruthless Nintendo president, decided to task them with a small project to steer HAL back towards profitability. He wanted them to make a Game Boy platformer starring a new mascot. Yamauchi's mission was accomplished with aplomb; from the moment you open your Game Boy to play *Kirby's Dream Land*, Kirby is a fully realized mascot in a game accessible to everyone.

The title screen features a lineup of multiple Kirbys jumping, making faces, doing a bit of moonwalking, generally being cute as hell. You immediately get a sense of joy emanating from this little character. Aside from wondering if there are multiple Kirbys in the world (an unresolved mystery we'll get back to shortly), you want to buy a plush Kirby just to hug it. As a first introduction its knocking it out of the park. Everything that makes Kirby lovely is there from the first moment except for its seminal copying ability which would appear in the second game. The game even manages to introduce musical themes that are still used today. As a matter of fact the

Kirby series has not only kept its songs, it kept its composer; Ishikawa Jun has always been the main composer for Kirby titles. I also want to give kudos to the sound designers for the very fun aspirating sound. Kirby sounds exactly like a vacuum, and it's perfect. Not everything is perfect but they clearly spent a lot of energy where it mattered for this game.

A Short Look at the Game That Reflects the Brevity of the Game

Here are some elements of the game's design that reflect a thoughtful design process and that will enhance your experience. If you play the game, and wonder why it's such a great little experience, then these choices explain the great fun you're having. It's incredible that so many magnificent design decisions were taken by a team led by such a young developer.

Graphics on Game Boy require a lot of foresight and planning to work well on the original Game Boy screen because its ghosting can make complicated graphics too difficult to see. *Kirby's Dream Land* showcases how to create beautiful graphics that still limit the amount of ghosting and keeping the game legible in all scenarios. It amounts to using a healthy dose of whitespace with discrete elements of characters and scenery drawn with thick borders but sparse internal details. Just like Kirby, most everything in the game is a shape with very little internal detail.

Another element that really helps the fidelity of Kirby's world is the belt scrolling. Belt scrolling describes a locked screen able to move in only one direction with the other axis locked. The screen can move left to right but it will not move up or down and it will not reverse either. If you imagine a level as if it's painted on an industrial belt, the crank to turn the belt can only go in one direction. Since you're only

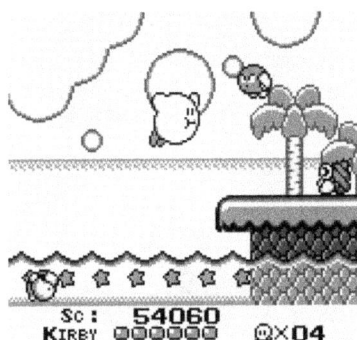

scrolling in one plane at a time (most often in this game from left to right) the ghosting is limited to streaks going in one direction. That helps a lot since you get accustomed to the predictable unidirectional ghosting. You don't think about it but it makes a big difference that ghosting streaks are mostly coming from a single direction.

Every stage starts with a short scene of Kirby getting his comeuppance from benign situations. Here Kirby runs after a butterfly that gets its buddies to fight back.

There is this saying amongst video game developers that if given a chance players will optimize the fun out of a game. What this means is that if developers give players a cheesy strategy players will use that advantage even if it makes the game boring to play for them. Developers have to account for this fact when designing a game and eliminate any strategies

Kirby tries fishing; it gets a mouthful of its own hook and falls in the water.

that make playtime boring. Flying in a platformer definitely falls under that axiom; what fun is there in a game where you can fly above every obstacle and eliminate any challenge? You might have fun for a couple of minutes due to the novelty but the appeal wears off quickly. *Super Mario World* is the golden reference when it comes to a platformer with flying elements. You can fly in the game which could potentially ruin the fun and make the game boring. To keep the game somewhat fun even if you skip levels with the cape you are required a lot of effort to maintain flight. It's not a simple one button process, meaning you will always have to do something. I don't feel it's a perfect solution since a repetitive task is never as fun as running through a gauntlet designed by the very best level designers in the world.

Kirby's Dream Land has Kirby flying indefinitely if you inhale air. It is a dead simple one-button move, which could definitely ruin the fun. Future games in the series will slow down Kirby's flight speed and agility, and limit your flight time. There are no such limitations here; Kirby is legitimately flying fast by flapping its tiny little arms. However, the game is not optimizing the fun out of the platforming like *Super Mario World*.

```
Sc: 60720
KIRBY ○○ · · · ·    ◎×05
```

How? The solution to the problem is actually wonderful because it uses the limitations of the Game Boy as a positive. Since the Game Boy has a limited resolution the play area in a platformer is small. In the case of *Kirby's Dream Land*, the play area is around eight Kirbys tall. Compared to a game on a CRT that's a very small play field above your characters' head. The smaller play field, which cannot scroll up, keeps the player involved because Kirby cannot fly very high. You just hover close to the ground always under the threat of a jumping enemy hitting you. The game also includes many enemies who loiter around the top of the screen, giving you obstacles to avoid even when you're in the air. So the small Game Boy screen actually makes a game more fun for once!

Unique in Scale and Scope

```
SOUND TEST

►MUSIC 00
▷SOUND 00
```

The game is simple and short, and unique in that regard. There are so few platformers like it. *Kirby's Dream Land* does not have a save function but it doesn't matter. You can easily clear the game in less than an hour. Anytime I think of a short platformer all the titles that come to mind are on Game Boy, with the exception of *A Short Hike*. I ask you, what is wrong with a game you can finish in an hour? Is there anything fundamentally wrong with an hour-long game? There isn't, it's simply a different artistic object. Not every platformer has to be extremely long, not every game has to stretch into infinity until you're bored out of your head. Even the further adventures of Kirby would turn into long games immediately after this game with *Kirby's Adventure* being a long-ass title requiring many hours to complete. It's unfortunate that we were collectively offered ever longer games. We could have had tons of fun platformers like *A Short Hike* for decades but instead everything had to be way too long all in the name of value. Ultimately, I hope we see more platformers akin to *Bowser's Fury* in the future; a clear concept that's fun for around two hours. I sincerely hope that it is the future of platformers as a genre; *Mario's Odyssey* was way too long and meandering. Platformers could benefit from the unique experiences that a short puzzle game like *Unpacking* provides.

If you want to play the game and you want a more involved challenge, try the bonus mode. It's properly difficult.

Marketing Meets Aesthetic

There's a link between the game's presentation and its difficulty. Because it's a short and easy title, it needs to tell potential buyers subconsciously. *A Short Hike* does it by literally being called a short hike. There's no question that this game is not meant to be difficult or long. *Kirby's Dream Land* features a cute character, usually a way to say that a game is for younger players. It also used the word dream in the title, which shouldn't imply something challenging. *Kirby's Nightmare Hellscape* calls to mind something much different: a difficult gauntlet with demons and guns. Basically, I think of *Doom*. I guess they ended up putting the word nightmare in the title of the remade version of *Kirby's Adventure* for Game Boy Advance, *Kirby: Nightmare in Dream Land*, but by that point Kirby was a well-known and popular character. They didn't need to signal as strongly what to expect with the marketing. *Kirby's Dream Land* was a smash hit in no small part due to its marketing and themes. It's an easy platformer kids will love but it's so well made that everyone should play it.

Conclusion

Kirby's Dream Land could only happen on Game Boy. It's a very short game featuring very little in the way of difficultly. Because of that it's the first game I ever finished.

When I was a kid, I owned two platformers at opposite ends of the Game Boy spectrum: *Donkey Kong Land* and *Kirby's Dream Land*. I have already talked about *Donkey Kong Land* and its atrocious choices. It's a terrible game for the limited Game Boy screen that ignores the shortcomings of the screen. *Kirby's Dream Land*, released three years earlier, is in contrast a wonderful game for the unique screen of the Game Boy. It respects the limits of the portable system's little green screen and creates a memorable game that sets the stage for a new mascot still popular to this day. If HAL Laboratory had not respected the limits imposed on them by the Game Boy we wouldn't be talking about Kirby anymore, and Sakurai probably would not have become Nintendo's biggest star developer of the 2010s.

The game even has a proper ending that rewards your efforts.
Kirby turns into a hot air balloon!

Oh, I totally forgot! I was supposed to get back to the mystery of the many Kirbys! When you finish the game, during the ending cinematic, Kirby can be seen dropping on a stage with a crowd barely visible at the bottom of the screen. They're all perfectly round shapes, only seen in shadows, which leads me to believe that Kirby was envisioned as the member of a whole species of Kirbys. They seemed to have abandoned that idea.

www.ingramcontent.com/pod-product-compliance
Lightning Source LLC
Chambersburg PA
CBHW071556200326
41519CB00021BB/6773